*This book is dedicated to the memory of all the suffragettes and suffragists
who did right and persisted knowing Failure Was Impossible.*

Consultant: June Purvis, Emeritus Professor of Women's
and Gender History at the University of Portsmouth, England

The author would like to thank
Suzanne Carnell, Lynn Roberts Maloney, June Purvis,
Chris Inns, Becky Chilcott, Helen Weir, Anita Anand, Crystal N. Feimster,
Jenny Shone, Ros Ball, Regina Marxer, and Chris Williams
for their help, guidance, and involvement in the making of this book.

Copyright © 2018, 2019 by David Roberts
Foreword copyright © 2019 by Crystal N. Feimster

First U.S. edition 2019
First published by Two Hoots an imprint of Pan Macmillan (U.K.) 2018

Library of Congress Catalog Card Number 2019939255
ISBN 978-1-5362-0841-2

19 20 21 22 23 24 WKT 10 9 8 7 6 5 4 3 2 1

Printed in Shenzhen, Guangdong, China

This book was typeset in ITC Usherwood and Scala Sans Pro.
The illustrations were done in watercolor, ink, and pencil on hot-pressed 300 gsm paper.

Walker Books US
a division of
Candlewick Press
99 Dover Street
Somerville, Massachusetts 02144

www.walkerbooksus.com

SUFFRAGETTE
THE BATTLE FOR EQUALITY

David Roberts

WALKER BOOKS

CONTENTS

Foreword

THE SEVENTY-FIVE-YEAR-LONG CAMPAIGN FOR WOMEN'S SUFFRAGE IN AMERICA AND BRITAIN IS ONE OF THE MOST IMPORTANT POLITICAL MOVEMENTS IN HISTORY. DETERMINED TO EXERCISE THEIR FULL RIGHTS AS CITIZENS, HUNDREDS OF THOUSANDS OF WOMEN PETITIONED, CANVASSED, LOBBIED, DEMONSTRATED, ENGAGED IN MASS CIVIL DISOBEDIENCE, WENT TO JAIL, AND PARTICIPATED IN HUNGER STRIKES FOR THE RIGHT TO VOTE.

In America the movement for women's suffrage officially began in 1848, when abolitionists Elizabeth Cady Stanton and Lucretia Mott organized the first women's rights convention in Seneca Falls, New York. Three hundred women and men, including the famous abolitionist Frederick Douglass, attended the convention. Many early suffragists were abolitionists who saw a connection between black emancipation from slavery and women's rights.

In England, the organized movement for women's suffrage began in 1866, when 1,499 British women and men, including Barbara Bodichon, Elizabeth Garrett, and John Stuart Mill, signed a petition to parliament insisting on women's suffrage.

In the early twentieth century, after decades of peacefully organizing, passing resolutions, signing petitions, lobbying politicians, penning letters to parliament, and testifying before committees, suffragists embraced more aggressive tactics.

In 1903, British suffragist Emmeline Pankhurst founded the Women's Social and Political Union (WSPU) under the slogan "Deeds, Not Words." Committed to civil disobedience, members of the WSPU broke windows, threw rocks, burned post offices, and cut telephone wires. They were dragged through the streets by the police. They starved themselves in prison and endured brutal force-feedings.

Such militant tactics might have remained largely confined to Britain if Alice Paul, an American Quaker from New Jersey, had not traveled to study in England and joined the WSPU. When Paul returned to the United States, she introduced American suffragists to the radical strategies she had learned from British suffragettes. Paul's borrowing of tactics was a reflection of the relationships and connections between suffragists of the period. Pankhurst traveled to the U.S. on several occasions to speak and to raise money.

The International Woman Suffrage Alliance, founded in 1904, offered women from many countries a platform to discuss their respective movements. While campaigns for women's suffrage began in the mid-nineteenth century in European countries, the U.S., New Zealand, and Australia, the right to vote was granted much earlier in some places than others. In New

Zealand, women gained the vote in 1893, while women in Greece had to wait until 1952.

Even though there were strong relationships between British and American suffragists, the movements were different in many ways. In the U.S., for example, before women eventually pursued the constitutional amendment that passed in 1920, many believed that the best strategy was to get the vote one state at a time. In Britain, by contrast, the campaign was more singularly focused on the parliamentary vote.

Racial and class dynamics also differed between the two countries. In both countries the national movements were led by white women, but suffragists of color, such as Sojourner Truth and Ida B. Wells-Barnett in the United States, and Princess Sophia Duleep Singh and Herabai Tata and her daughter Mithan Lam in Britain and its colonies, organized and worked tirelessly for women's suffrage.

However, in America race was the most divisive issue within the movement. The franchise had been extended to almost all white male citizens by 1856. The Fourteenth and Fifteenth Amendments granted the franchise to African American men but specifically excluded women. After the passage of the Fifteenth Amendment in 1870, many white suffragists, including abolitionists such as Susan B. Anthony, appealed to white supremacy as a rationale for giving white women the vote.

African American women were often denied admission into the major suffrage organizations and meetings. In 1913, when Alice Paul organized the first national suffrage parade in Washington, DC, she relegated black suffragists to the back of the parade. Ida B. Wells-Barnett, founder of the Alpha Suffrage Club for black women in Chicago, refused to be segregated and marched with white suffragists at the front.

While the suffrage movement in Britain was also made up largely of white women, class, not race, played a more pronounced role in their campaigns. By 1866, suffrage in Britain was based not only on gender, but also on ownership of property. Thus, given the exclusion of non-propertied working-class men from the electorate, "Votes for Women" in England often meant votes for propertied women.

Working-class women, however, played a key role in the movement for women's suffrage. In 1912, Annie Kenney became the first and only working-class woman appointed to a senior position in the WSPU. Nevertheless, when the Representation of the People Act passed in 1918, only women over thirty years of age who owned property or whose husbands were property owners were given the franchise.

Even though all American women won the right to vote with the passage of the Nineteenth Amendment in 1920, black women who lived in the American South were still denied the franchise. Subject to poll taxes, literacy tests, and threats of violence, black women and men remained disenfranchised until the passage of the Voting Rights Act of 1965.

Born in 1972, I was a beneficiary of not only the women's suffrage movement, but also the civil rights and women's rights movements of the 1960s. I grew up with Susan B. Anthony dollar coins in my pocket and celebrating Martin Luther King Jr.'s birthday as a national holiday. As a college student in the 1990s, I was taught the history of the women's suffrage movement and introduced to many of the women beautifully illustrated in *Suffragette*. Their stories of courage, determination, and the relentless struggle for women's equality inspired my own feminist politics and commitment to women's rights.

A gorgeous and breathtaking introduction to the women's suffrage movement, *Suffragette* celebrates these brave women who changed the world.

Crystal N. Feimster, PhD
New Haven, Connecticut

Introduction

U NTIL I WAS FOURTEEN YEARS OLD, I HAD
NEVER HEARD OF THE SUFFRAGETTES.

The year was 1984, and my history teacher, Mrs. Pile, informed the class that for our end-of-year exam we had to write and illustrate a project on a topic we had studied during the year. Had I heard right? Illustrate! I was thrilled: anything that meant I could draw was a bonus.

A collection of faded old history books on a variety of subjects was scattered on the teacher's desk, and one by one each student went up to choose a book on which to base their project. Amid the books about famous British historical figures such as Humphry Davy, Edward Jenner, and Isambard Kingdom Brunel was a book that caught my eye. It had a black-and-white photograph on the cover showing two women in prison uniform: dark dresses covered in white arrows, aprons tied around their waists, mobcaps on their heads. They stood arm in arm, and above them was the title: *The Suffragettes*.

Who were these people? What was a "suffragette"? And what terrible crime had they committed to be sent to prison? I took the book eagerly and turned straight to the middle where the pictures were. Slowly the story revealed itself.

These were Edwardian ladies of the early 1900s who had protested and battled with the government of their day to win the vote. They had smashed stuff up, burned stuff down, and even died to be given equal political rights with men. I was captivated. Their struggle for equality really spoke to me.

Most of my friends were girls, but I am sure back then not many of them would have called themselves feminists. Being a teenage boy, I certainly didn't realize I could call *myself* a feminist. But I had a very strong sense of injustice at the way boys and girls were treated differently.

In those days, the gender divide was still very stark: at school, boys played soccer while girls played netball; girls did needlework while boys did metalwork. Why? I would have been much more at home in the needlework class than doing metalwork, and I know that some of my female friends longed to be on the soccer team. But those options just weren't available to us, or if they were, not many people would want to stand out by choosing them.

The expectation for boys and girls to fit into their gender stereotypes seemed ridiculous and unfair. One friend of mine who did proudly call herself a feminist would always speak out if she felt she was being dismissed, stereotyped, or patronized because she was a girl, but often her protests were met with groans from teachers and pupils alike.

Our class had never studied the suffragettes in history, or in any other lesson for that matter, so I have no idea why that book was on the teacher's desk. It's a mystery. But it started in me a lifelong interest and respect for this group of women who had stood up to the men in power and begun to change the way society viewed their gender and the way it restricted their lives, ambitions, and right to be seen as equal citizens with one another and with men.

More than thirty years after I wrote my school project, I have delved back into the history and learned so much more about the campaign for women's suffrage. Of course, illustrating this book has been enormous fun,

researching amid the treasure trove of newspaper reports, photographs, posters, and postcards that the Internet has made readily available. I have interpreted some of these images to make my own illustrations and have enjoyed visualizing scenes from some of the stories I've read for which there were no photographs.

These stories include that of Miss Spark and Miss Shaw barricading themselves at the top of the Monument tower in London to unfurl a massive banner that read DEATH OR VICTORY before showering the astounded crowds below with hundreds of pamphlets declaring VOTES FOR WOMEN. Of the fearless Muriel Matters being pelted with rotten fish as she gave a speech in front of a rowdy crowd of men. The stories illustrated here are mostly of British suffrage campaigners, but I've included Americans, too, and tried to show how the campaigns were linked.

I am not an expert, but more of an enthusiast—inspired by a diverse group of people, both suffragists and suffragettes, courageous, determined, peaceful, and militant, all focused on one thing: the right to vote.

One hundred years since women first won the right to vote, we continue to challenge ourselves on gender equality and the expectations and roles of women and men. Slowly we chip away at the limitations and barriers to equality that previous generations and many people still today suffered and suffer. Femininity does not equal weakness, and gender equality benefits everyone.

The campaigners for women's suffrage understood that. Here are some of their extraordinary stories.

David Roberts

A Man's World

So WHY WEREN'T WOMEN ALLOWED TO VOTE? IT'S SAD TO SAY, BUT THROUGHOUT HISTORY, IN THE UNITED KINGDOM, THE UNITED STATES, AND MANY OTHER PLACES AROUND THE WORLD, WOMEN AND GIRLS WERE CONSIDERED WEAK AND EVEN SILLY, ABLE ONLY TO BRING UP CHILDREN AND BE GOOD HOUSEWIVES.

A woman wasn't believed capable of making major decisions about her own life, let alone about the way her country should be governed. Men were expected to make those decisions. Men were expected to be in charge. So men took control and made all the rules. Often the rules they made favored other men who were just like them, however unfair that might be. For instance, even by the mid-nineteenth century, the Victorians didn't bother to educate girls the same way they would educate boys. Some girls would have some sort of education, but only if they were rich and either went to a private girls' school or had a governess to teach them at home. Education was expensive and served primarily as a path to a profession, a career, and an intellectual mind: the things *boys* needed to succeed in life, not considered the concern of girls.

In 1870, a law was passed in the U.K. that made school

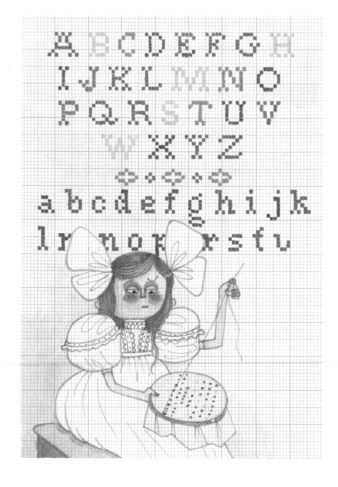

free. In 1880, schooling was made compulsory up to the age of ten, then eleven in 1893, and fourteen in 1899. It wasn't until 1918 that every state in the U.S. had a compulsory education law. But these laws did not offer as much progress for girls as you might think. Girls were often kept at home on washdays or other days to help around the house. And it isn't just going to school but what's being taught there that matters. In addition to reading, writing, and arithmetic, girls traditionally learned cookery, needlework, and general domestic duties: all great skills, but if they are seen as "girl only" subjects, then it's clear that girls are being trained chiefly to be good housewives, while the boys are being encouraged to expand their minds and prepare for adult life beyond the home.

As time went on, girls' education did get better, but progress was frustratingly slow. University or college spots for women were rare, and even if a woman did get accepted to study a subject like medicine or law, which for a man might become his profession, she couldn't work as a doctor or a lawyer after she graduated. Women in the U.K. weren't allowed to be doctors until 1876 or lawyers until 1922. In the United States, a woman first received a medical degree in 1849, and a woman was first admitted to the bar in 1869.

But a university education was out of reach for most people, women and men: only the wealthy could afford it. For the majority of the population, life was tough. Men and women worked long hours as servants or in factories, in mines or as farm laborers. The work was not only hard but often dangerous, and pay was low.

To make matters worse, a woman would be paid a lower wage than a man, even if she was doing the same job. And after a hard day's work, she still had to clean and cook at home.

But unequal pay, an issue even today, was just one of many shocking inequalities for women at this time.

If a woman got married, she had to promise to "obey" her husband in her marriage vows, but a man never had to promise to obey his wife. A married woman gave up what few rights she had when she was single: her husband "owned" her. He also owned all her wealth and property. Even if the home they lived in had belonged to her before her marriage, her husband could throw her out on the street without a penny if he wanted to divorce her. She, on the other hand, could not even divorce him without his agreement.

A British woman had no legal rights over her own children until 1839, when a law was passed to give women the right to apply for custody (or guardianship) of children under the age of seven. The same law also gave women the right to apply for access to her children over the age of seven. Before this, if a marriage broke up, a father could take their children away from their mother and legally deny her the right to ever see them again. Courts in the U.S. followed British practice in these matters.

Thankfully, many people realized these laws were wrong, and by the end of the nineteenth century most of the worst old laws that discriminated against women were gone. Women were gradually gaining more control over their lives.

Yet still they were not equal citizens with men. In the U.K., they were not allowed to vote in parliamentary elections. In the U.S., their ability to vote in elections was determined by the state they lived in. Most states didn't allow it. Some men thought this was the way things should stay. Most surprisingly, some women thought so too.

But by the time the Victorian era ended with the death of the queen in 1901, one group of people had been for many years asking the question "Why can't women vote?" Recognizing that nothing would change fundamentally for women until they could take part in elections, this group began to demand that the government give them the vote. These people were called suffragists.

What Is Suffrage?

SUFFRAGISTS ARE THOSE WHO CAMPAIGN FOR THE RIGHT TO VOTE, EITHER FOR THEMSELVES OR FOR OTHERS.

Suffragist comes from the word *suffrage,* which means the right to vote in political elections. The right to vote is sometimes also called the *franchise.*

Using your franchise, or voting, is important because it is a way of expressing your choice or point of view when a decision is being made on which a group of people have different opinions. A democracy is a system of government in which everyone should have an equal right to express his or her point of view.

Today, the United Kingdom and the United States are democracies. In the U.K., there is a parliamentary election called a general election at least every five years. Everyone over the age of eighteen is asked to vote for a member of Parliament (MP). Everyone is free to vote for an MP they think will best represent their point of view in Parliament on the big decisions about how we live our lives. In the U.S., the vote for a new president happens every four years, and there are

elections for local, state, and federal representatives of different kinds every year.

Things were not always done this way. Throughout history (and still today in some places), people have had to fight and struggle to be given the right to vote on equal terms with others.

For a very long time in the United Kingdom and the United States, women were not allowed to vote in elections, so they had no say in how their countries were governed. They had no way of expressing a political view or of influencing the laws under which they lived. They were denied suffrage.

It was indeed a man's world . . . but not for all men equally. It wasn't a simple case that all men could vote and no women could. For many years, millions of men were also denied the right to vote. It took a long time, many riots, violence, and petitions to the government before things started to change.

To better understand the story, we need to travel back in time to the Middle Ages.

Centuries ago, Britain was ruled by a king, and he alone made decisions for the people. But the king needed the support of the noblemen and landowners who paid him taxes, and over time these men decided that they should have a say in how the country was run.

This eventually led to the creation of a permanent parliament in which the noblemen voted and made the laws.

Most people living in Britain were not noblemen; they were ordinary working people. And they had no vote.

So all the decisions about how most people lived their lives were being made by a very small, privileged group. This was not full democracy.

As time passed, many of the "ordinary" people, fed up with such injustice, demanded their right to a vote as well.

In the late 1700s in America, people broke from the monarchy entirely, fighting for and forming a new country and declaring that all men were equal. They meant just white men, though.

I will be your leader some day

Another huge change happened in 1832, when a decision was made in the British Parliament to allow more men to vote. This was called the Great Reform Act. Although it was a step in the right direction, it only allowed more wealthy men to vote and still excluded millions of other men—and all women.

In the U.S., the Fifteenth Amendment to the Constitution was ratified in 1870, giving African American men—freed from slavery after the Civil War—the right to vote.

By 1867 in Britain, more and more people were demanding suffrage. A decision was made to give men who owned their own homes the right to vote. This was the Second Reform Act, but it still excluded many working men—and all women.

By 1884 in Britain, the fight for universal suffrage was growing even stronger. The government passed the Third Reform Act, giving many more men the right to a parliamentary vote, but it still excluded millions of working-class men—and all women.

Some MPs had tried to persuade the prime minister, William Gladstone, to give women the vote. But although he was not entirely against the idea, he believed there was not enough support for it in Parliament, and that the law would not be passed at all if women were included.

Gladstone was probably right. Queen Victoria herself wrote to him, cautioning against this "mad folly of women's rights," a view still commonly held at the time.

But the suffragists were not about to give up, and the campaign for votes for women was getting steadily more powerful in Britain and the United States.

1832: The Vote Lost

BUT WAIT! HAD SOME WOMEN BEEN ALLOWED TO VOTE MANY YEARS AGO?

Some suffragists believed they had, and that in their campaign for votes for women, they were fighting not for something new but for something that had been taken from them.

It was known that long ago in Anglo-Saxon England, an abbess (the woman in charge of an abbey) had been involved in law-making. Saint Hild of Whitby was a powerful abbess. She founded an abbey that was home to both nuns and monks. Historical documents showed that Saint Hild had been engaged in the politics of her time, involved in discussions with the king in the year 664 about when Easter should be set in the calendar year.

Politicians who wrote this new law in 1832 used the words "male persons" to indicate who was now allowed to vote. Previously the word used was "mankind," a word often understood to describe both men and women.

In 1867, a clerical error did add one woman's name to the electoral register: Lily Maxwell, a shopkeeper from Manchester, England.

When it came to the attention of the local suffrage groups that Lily had been accidentally registered to vote, they made sure she did just that, and on November 26, 1867, Lily Maxwell became the first woman to vote in a parliamentary election since the law had changed in 1832.

Her pioneering action prompted more than 5,000 women who owned property in and around the Manchester area to try to register their names on the electoral roll in 1868. All of them were rejected.

Some suffragists also believed that later, in Tudor times (the 1500s), women in England who owned land had voted in parliamentary elections.

If that is true, then it means the right to vote was taken away from women by the introduction of the Great Reform Act.

But the fight for women's suffrage was beginning in earnest—a fight that was to last another sixty years before women would be able to vote on equal terms with men.

1832–1897: The Acorn Becomes a Mighty Oak

WOMEN HAVE BEEN STRIVING FOR EQUAL RIGHTS WITH MEN FOR HUNDREDS OF YEARS, BUT BY 1832, STILL VERY FEW PEOPLE, MEN OR WOMEN, WERE IN FAVOR OF GIVING WOMEN THE RIGHT TO VOTE IN ELECTIONS.

But one person in England who did think it was important decided to write a petition to Parliament. Her name was Mary Smith.

A petition is like a letter to the government asking it to do something. Mary pointed out that as a woman, she had to live by the exact same laws as men and pay taxes just as they did, so why should she not be able to vote, just as they did? Without a vote, she had no influence over either laws or taxes, which was completely unfair. Most MPs thought this was just a joke, and in 1832, no one took Mary seriously at all.

In 1866, a group of women in the U.K. called the Kensington Society decided to write their own petition. They included Barbara Bodichon, Emily Davies, and Elizabeth Garrett. They had friends who were MPs: John Stuart Mill and Henry Fawcett, both of whom supported votes for women. John Stuart Mill agreed to take the petition to Parliament.

If you want to get your petition noticed, you need people to sign it—lots of people. The Kensington Society's petition had 1,499 signatures of women, rich and poor, from all across Britain. Teachers, dressmakers, shopkeepers, scientists, mathematicians, servants, and many wealthy ladies all signed it. But the government took no notice.

Imagine how frustrated those women must have felt when only a year later the law changed to give 938,427 more men the vote—but still no women.

In 1867, the Kensington Society became the London Society for Women's Suffrage. This was the beginning of a properly organized women's suffrage movement. Soon more and more societies appeared all over the country.

This did not amuse Queen Victoria, who in 1870 declared, "Let women be what God intended, a Helpmate for Man." But this only made the suffragists even more determined to win.

In 1897, seventeen suffrage societies in the U.K. joined up to make one big group called the National Union of Women's Suffrage Societies (NUWSS). Their first president was a wise and powerful woman named Millicent Garrett Fawcett.

Millicent Garrett Fawcett

MILLICENT GARRETT (LATER MILLICENT GARRETT FAWCETT) WAS BORN IN 1847. SHE WAS ONE OF TEN CHILDREN.

As a girl, Millicent enjoyed reading and learning, and she was sent to boarding school in London. As she grew up, she became interested in the education of girls and women, and in how unequal their education was to that of most boys and men. For example, her older sister, Elizabeth Garrett (later Elizabeth Garrett Anderson), had found it difficult to find a college where a woman could study to become a doctor. But Elizabeth didn't give up, and went on to become Britain's first female doctor.

Another of her sisters, Louise, introduced Millicent to many interesting people who had forward-thinking views on women's rights. In 1865, they went to hear a speech given by the MP John Stuart Mill. Millicent was captivated by his progressive ideas and belief that women should have equal rights with men. This was a shocking view to hold at the time.

In 1867, Millicent married the MP Henry Fawcett, himself an avid supporter of women's rights. Henry was blind, and Millicent would act as his eyes by writing down speeches and debates that took place in Parliament. She spent many hours sitting in the Ladies' Gallery, the part

of the House of Commons where women were allowed to go to watch the proceedings. She didn't much like the Ladies' Gallery. It was hot and stuffy and gave her a headache. But by now, Millicent had a keen interest in politics herself and wrote books and essays on the subject.

She became an outstanding person in the campaign to win votes for women. Although she didn't much like public speaking (in fact, it made her feel sick), she gave many speeches, not only about votes for women but also about education and the rights of working women. Millicent knew that if women gained the vote, it would be a stepping-stone toward changing many of the terrible ways they were being treated in the home and the workplace.

As the leader of the NUWSS, the biggest of all the women's suffrage societies, she insisted that its members campaign peacefully, within the law, but relentlessly. She always maintained this was the only way to achieve public and government support to win the vote.

When women in the U.K. finally won full equal voting rights with men, Millicent had been peacefully campaigning for sixty-one years.

MARY SMITH (CA. EARLY 1800s)
In 1832 she was the first woman
to petition the government for the right to vote,
arguing that since women paid taxes to the
government, they should be allowed to vote for it.

ELIZABETH WOLSTENHOLME-ELMY (1833–1918)
A campaigner for girls' education and a member of the
Kensington Society, and later a member of the Women's
Social and Political Union, she refused to "obey" in her
marriage vows, to wear a ring, or to give up her surname.

LYDIA BECKER (1827–1890)
An amateur scientist interested in botany and astronomy,
she founded the *Women's Suffrage Journal*. In 1880 she
was involved in the successful campaign for women to
vote in Isle of Man parliamentary elections.

JOHN STUART MILL (1806–1873)
A politician and campaigner for gender equality, he
was the first MP to call for giving women the vote.
He is now perhaps best known as a philosopher who
believed in the importance of individual liberty.

British Suffragists and Their Supporters

SUPPORTERS OF WOMEN'S SUFFRAGE IN THE U.K. FORMED MANY GROUPS, UNIONS, AND FEDERATIONS, MOST OF WHICH WERE NONVIOLENT.

Eighteen of these groups joined forces to create the biggest British women's suffrage organization, the NUWSS, whose members were known as suffragists. Their tactics, unlike those of the suffragettes who would follow, were focused on campaigning within the law. By 1914, their more restrained style had attracted about 55,000 members to join the union once described as "a glacier, slow moving but unstoppable."

But not all the suffragist groups acted within the law. The Men's Political Union for Women's Enfranchisement (MPU) and the Women's Freedom League (WFL) both had militant activists among their members, including those who smashed windows or refused to pay taxes.

HUGH FRANKLIN (1889–1962)
A member of the Men's League for Woman's Suffrage
and Jewish League for Woman Suffrage, he was a militant
activist who was imprisoned and force-fed 114 times. He
married WSPU member Elsie Duval, sister of Victor.

CHARLOTTE DESPARD (1844–1939)
A novelist and a founder of both the Women's Freedom
League and the Irish Women's Franchise League, she was
a pacifist who encouraged militant protest and
was imprisoned more than once.

VICTOR DUVAL (1885–1945)
Husband of the suffragette Una Dugdale, he founded
the militant Men's Political Union for Women's
Enfranchisement and was a member of the
International Women's Franchise Club.

CATHERINE IMPEY (1847–1923)
A Quaker, vegetarian, and women's suffrage supporter,
she founded Britain's first anti-racism journal, *Anti-Caste*,
and arranged for a British lecture tour by U.S. civil rights
campaigner Ida B. Wells-Barnett.

HENRY FAWCETT (1833–1884)
A politician, he was the husband of Millicent Garrett
Fawcett and one of the earliest campaigners for women's
rights. He was blinded in a shooting accident at the
age of twenty-five.

MURIEL MATTERS (1877–1969)
Australian born, she was a member of the Women's
Freedom League, famous for her fearless publicity
stunts. A journalist, lecturer, actress, and educator,
she ran for Parliament in 1924.

WILLIAM BALL (CA. LATE 1800s)
With jobs ranging from gardener to master tailor,
he was one of the few men to become a militant activist.
Often imprisoned, he was force-fed more than
one hundred times.

TERESA BILLINGTON-GREIG (1877–1964)
A teacher, journalist, and writer of books on women's
rights, she was a key organizer of the Women's Freedom
League and frequently imprisoned. She and husband
Frederick Greig joined their surnames on marriage.

LUCRETIA MOTT (1793–1880)
As a Quaker, she believed all people were equal. She was a preacher and well-regarded public speaker for the abolitionist cause. As Elizabeth Cady Stanton's mentor, she remained a leader in the women's suffrage movement throughout her long life and cofounded Swarthmore College for women and men.

SOJOURNER TRUTH (CA. 1797–1883)
A Methodist preacher, former slave, abolitionist, and speaker, she gave one of the most famous speeches of the suffrage movement, refuting a man who claimed women were too helpless to vote. She said, in part: "I could work as much and eat as much as a man—when I could get it—and bear the lash as well! And ain't I a woman?" This final phrase became a rallying cry of the cause.

Notable U.S. Suffragists

THROUGHOUT THE YEARS OF THE BRITISH SUFFRAGE MOVEMENT, THE UNITED STATES WAS ALSO EXPERIENCING A TIME OF GREAT SOCIAL AND INDUSTRIAL CHANGE. AS MANY NEW FACTORIES SPRUNG UP, MORE WOMEN WERE TAKING JOBS OUTSIDE THE HOME. OTHERS WERE FINDING LEADERSHIP ROLES IN THE NEWER PROTESTANT DENOMINATIONS LIKE QUAKERISM AND METHODISM, WHICH ENCOURAGED WOMEN TO PREACH IN PUBLIC. MEETING SO MANY LIKE-MINDED WOMEN AT WORK AND IN CHURCH, THEY BEGAN TO FORM LABOR UNIONS AND SOCIETIES FOR MORAL AND SOCIAL IMPROVEMENT. MANY ALSO JOINED GROUPS LIKE THE AMERICAN ANTI-SLAVERY SOCIETY.

It was at the World Anti-Slavery Convention of 1840 in London that two women who would become leaders of the U.S. women's suffrage movement first met: Lucretia Mott and Elizabeth Cady Stanton. The two Americans had crossed an ocean to participate, but were not allowed to speak at the convention because of their sex. They instead had to sit quietly in a separate gallery. The irony of a convention about freedom quashing the freedom of those in attendance was not lost on either woman, and they spent the rest of their time in London together, talking about the possibility of a women's rights convention. It would eventually take place in Seneca Falls, New York, in 1848, with Lucretia Mott as the top-billed speaker and Elizabeth Cady Stanton as the primary author of the Declaration of Sentiments, the proposal of resolutions to be voted on by the attendees. Stanton modeled it on the Declaration of Independence, the United States' founding document, and included a truly revolutionary resolution: that women should have the right to vote. This was the formal beginning of the American women's suffrage movement.

ELIZABETH CADY STANTON (1815–1902)

Born to a lawyer father who taught her how laws could be changed if deemed unjust, she became the leading figure in the early U.S. women's suffrage movement, helping to found the American Equal Rights Association (AERA), which fought for the vote for women and African American men. She saw that without the vote women couldn't change unfair laws. She later became a divisive figure whose racist sentiments led in part to a split in the movement.

CAROLINE G. PARKER MOUNTPLEASANT (CA. 1826–1892)

Born into a prominent Seneca (Iroquois) family—her brother was Ely S. Parker, a lieutenant colonel in the Union army and secretary to Ulysses S. Grant—Mountpleasant was fluent in English and Seneca, a talented craftsperson (her beadwork is in many museum collections), and, by tradition, a prominent leader in her tribe. Native American women such as Mountpleasant, whose nations gave them the right to hold political positions and own property, inspired early suffragists like Lucretia Mott, Elizabeth Cady Stanton, and Matilda Joslyn Gage.

FREDERICK DOUGLASS (1818–1895)

A newspaper owner, speaker, statesman, and former slave, he was one of the most prominent abolitionist figures and used his prominence to also advance the cause of women's rights. He was one of the few male attendees of the Seneca Falls Convention and helped convince others to support Elizabeth Cady Stanton's controversial resolution for women's suffrage.

FRANCIS ELLEN WATKINS HARPER (1825–1911)

A writer, poet, journalist, teacher, abolitionist, and suffragist, Harper published popular volumes of poetry on the black experience, making her one of the first African American women to be published. She held prominent roles in temperance, abolitionist, and suffrage organizations and was a powerful speaker on the particular plight of African American women, saying at the National Women's Rights Convention in 1866: "You white women here speak here of rights. I speak of wrongs. I, as a colored woman, have had in this country an education which has made me feel as if I were in the situation of Ishmael, my hand against every man, and every man's hand against me."

SUSAN B. ANTHONY (1820–1906)

A Quaker, teacher, and leader in the temperance movement to make alcohol illegal in the U.S., she became Elizabeth Cady Stanton's greatest ally and friend. She traveled tirelessly, speaking and circulating petitions to grow support for the cause of women's suffrage, and at a time when it was unusual and dangerous for a woman to travel alone. She voted illegally in the 1872 presidential election and was promptly arrested and put on trial. Her case brought national attention to the cause. Her leadership of the movement extended from its beginnings to its later national prominence—almost to its ultimate victory.

1903: The Time Is Now

ALTHOUGH THE MOVEMENT IN BRITAIN HAD GROWN, BY 1903 THE SUFFRAGISTS' PROGRESS WAS SLOW, AND ONE GROUP GREW INCREASINGLY IMPATIENT FOR CHANGE.

Some campaigners, like Millicent Fawcett and members of the NUWSS, continued to lobby the government to give women the vote by peacefully organizing petitions and encouraging MPs sympathetic to their cause to raise the subject in Parliament. But others, frustrated with the government's refusal to listen to them, felt ignored and overlooked. It was time for a defiant new voice to speak up. Emmeline Pankhurst had had enough of talking, which she felt was achieving nothing.

One evening in October 1903 at her home in Manchester, England, along with her eldest daughter, Christabel, and some like-minded local women, Emmeline formed a new women's suffrage group, the Women's Social and Political Union (WSPU). Anyone could join . . . as long as they were female. Unlike the NUWSS, no men were allowed to join as members, although they were welcome as supporters.

Men like Frederick Pethick-Lawrence, for example. His wife, another Emmeline, was a member of the WSPU and became honorary treasurer in 1906. Frederick and Emmeline believed in equality between men and women and even took each other's names in marriage. So Emmeline Pethick and Frederick Lawrence became Mr. and Mrs. Pethick-Lawrence, which made a very clear stand against the idea that a man "owned" his wife.

The Pethick-Lawrences later worked together as the editors of the WSPU's newspaper, *Votes for Women*, which was launched in 1907. By 1910, the circulation had risen to 30,000. It was being sold throughout the country, both through newsdealers and by individual members of the WSPU, who often had to stand in the gutter to do so, since standing on the sidewalk could be called an obstruction and might lead to their arrest. It was an excellent campaigning tool, spreading the message of the fight for women's suffrage through cartoons and articles; advertising forthcoming meetings and demonstrations; and reporting on the activities of WSPU members. It was a rallying cry to supporters and called for new members to join.

As a lawyer, Frederick Pethick-Lawrence also represented the WSPU in legal matters, including trials, because women were not allowed to do so. Christabel Pankhurst had a degree in law, but because she was a woman, she was not able to work in her field.

Christabel became the key strategist of the WSPU, and she and her mother set out the broad outlines of policy for the union. Individual members had considerable freedom to decide which acts they should engage in, be it working at the headquarters, taking part in protests, or just giving money to the WSPU; but the leaders set the tone.

Right from the start, the WSPU saw itself as an army and its members as soldiers, working together. All that was required was an unquestioning loyalty to the cause.

Many women liked this bold new approach and were attracted to the active spirit of the union. The WSPU's membership quickly swelled to make it an impressive fighting machine, a force to be reckoned with, led by the determined Emmeline Pankhurst.

Emmeline Pankhurst

BORN IN 1858, EMMELINE PANKHURST LEARNED ABOUT POLITICS FROM A YOUNG AGE.

As a child, Emmeline Goulden (as she was then) would read newspapers aloud to her father and, schoolbag in hand, accompany her mother to women's suffrage meetings. Both her parents held strong views in favor of women's rights.

She went to school in Manchester, England, and later in Paris, but Emmeline realized that her education was never taken as seriously as that of her brothers. Theirs focused on business, mathematics, science—subjects a boy could build a career on—whereas hers focused on domestic skills, such as how to keep a nice home and care for her family. Emmeline was indignant: Why should she be expected to keep a nice home for her brothers, while they were never expected to do the same for her?

One night, she overheard her father whisper to her mother, "What a pity she wasn't born a lad." Emmeline wanted to shout out in protest, "I don't want to be a boy!" But from then on she realized that the world saw men as superior to women—and she became increasingly determined to change that view.

In 1879, she married a lawyer, Dr. Richard Pankhurst, who was himself a radical thinker and strong supporter of women's rights. She became very interested in the lives of working-class women and, in 1888, lent her enthusiastic support to the Match Girl Strikes.

The match girls and women worked up to fourteen hours a day in a factory making safety matches. They were poorly paid and could be fined for something as minor as talking or even for going to the bathroom without permission. In addition, they suffered from poor health because they were exposed to phosphorus, a chemical used to make the matches. It made their skin turn bright yellow and their hair fall out. Worse still, it gave them a hideous bone-rotting disease called phossy jaw.

When the story of these truly appalling working conditions reached the newspapers, first in an article written by the campaigner Annie Besant, the factory bosses tried to force the women to sign a statement saying the reports were nonsense and that in fact they were all having a lovely time at work. Some refused to sign, and when the leader of that group was fired, 1,400 women and girls walked out on strike. The strike lasted three weeks, but by the time the women returned to work, their demands for better working conditions, including no more fines, were granted.

Emmeline saw just how powerful women could be by standing together to fight for their rights, and this spirit inspired her in the formation of the WSPU and throughout her days of campaigning.

Deeds No

1903

THE FIRST THING EMMELINE PANKHURST AND THE LEADERS OF THE BRAND-NEW WSPU DID WAS TO COME UP WITH THE BRILLIANT SLOGAN "DEEDS, NOT WORDS."

It was a phrase that would encourage and motivate, a rallying cry to women everywhere that the time for politely talking about votes for women was over. Now was the time for action! Time to get the job done. Emmeline Pankhurst said, "Women don't want to be lawbreakers, they want to be lawmakers!" But break the law they would.

LUCY STONE (1818–1893)

An abolitionist and professional speaker, she used her platform to protest slavery and advance women's rights. She led the AERA with Elizabeth Cady Stanton and Susan B. Anthony, but split with them over support of a Fifteenth Amendment to the U.S. Constitution, which gave African American men the right to vote ahead of women. Stone was willing to support the amendment and wait for women's chance; Stanton and Anthony were not and protested it.

MATILDA JOSLYN GAGE (1826–1898)

A speaker, writer, and newspaper owner, she was president of the National Woman Suffrage Association (NWSA), formed by Stanton and Anthony after their split with Lucy Stone. A prolific writer, she coauthored, with Stanton and Anthony, the first volumes of *History of Woman Suffrage*, which became an authoritative history of the movement. But because it was written from the perspective of white suffragists, it did not fully take in the efforts of African American suffragists. Gage also wrote extensively about Native Americans and what she saw as their more equitable gender traditions and laws.

CARRIE CHAPMAN CATT (1859–1947)

A school superintendent and reporter, she led the National American Woman Suffrage Association (NAWSA), a united organization formed in 1890 from the previously divided suffrage groups. She led the campaign to pass a referendum in Colorado to make it only the second state to give women the right to vote. She supported winning the vote state by state, a strategy that younger, more radical suffragists would rebel against. She founded the League of Women Voters in 1920 and helped found the International Woman Suffrage Alliance.

U.S. Suffragists and the Organized Movement

THE WOMEN'S SUFFRAGE MOVEMENT IN THE UNITED STATES GREW OUT OF THE ABOLITIONIST MOVEMENT TO END SLAVERY, WITH MANY EARLY SUFFRAGISTS ALSO ACTIVE ABOLITIONISTS.

But in the aftermath of the American Civil War, with slavery abolished, the causes of advancing the rights of women and people of color became divided over the issue of the Fifteenth Amendment, which would grant the franchise to African American men. The first national suffrage organization, the American Equal Rights Association (AERA), split into National Woman Suffrage Association (NWSA) and the American Woman Suffrage Association (AWSA) over whether the voting rights of women should have precedence over those of African American men. The rights of African American women were often overlooked in this discussion. It wasn't until 1890 that the two organizations re-formed into one national organization, the National American Woman Suffrage Association (NAWSA). Even then, black women were met with a mixed welcome, and not every NAWSA chapter allowed them to join. Some formed their own suffrage organizations, such as the Alpha Suffrage Club and the National Association of Colored Women (NACW).

ANNA JULIA COOPER (1858–1964)
A graduate of Oberlin College, Cooper was a celebrated educator at the M Street High School in Washington, DC, one of the first high schools for African Americans. She encouraged black students to pursue a college education when others believed vocational training was more appropriate. She became involved in the black women's club movement, a precursor to the National Association of Colored Women, and received a PhD from the Sorbonne in Paris for her dissertation on slavery.

IDA B. WELLS-BARNETT (1862–1931)
A newspaper owner and journalist, she risked her life to report on the practice of lynching, in which white Southerners would torture and hang African American men and boys for dubious crimes as a means of intimidation and suppression. Wells-Barnett also wrote and campaigned for women's suffrage, though without consistent support from white suffragists. She founded the Alpha Suffrage Club to give black women a voice in the movement, and refused to be relegated to the back of the first national suffrage parade.

ALICE PAUL (1885–1977)
While studying in London, she heard Christabel Pankhurst speak and was inspired to join the WSPU. She was arrested several times for her part in their protests and brought their confrontational tactics back to the U.S. suffrage movement, leading a provocative march on Washington in 1913 and the picketing of the White House for two straight years. She drafted the Equal Rights Amendment, which would give American women the right to equal treatment under law with men. This amendment has yet to be ratified.

LUCY BURNS (1879–1966)
She met Alice Paul when both American WSPU members were arrested in London. Back home they joined the NAWSA and pushed it, against Carrie Chapman Catt's guidance, to pursue a federal suffrage law in the form of a constitutional amendment rather than trying to win the vote state by state. Arrested and jailed while picketing the White House with Paul, she would protest in a hunger strike that would help win the sympathy of the country.

NANNIE HELEN BURROUGHS (1879–1961)
When she was denied a teaching job in Washington, DC, Burroughs opened her own school for black women and girls. She believed education, better paying jobs, and the right to vote were crucial to black women's advancement in society, and helped found the National Association of Colored Women, a women's rights organization created in part out of frustration with black women's lack of voice in predominantly white suffrage organizations.

1905: "The Question! The Question! Answer the Question!"

IT HAD ALL GOTTEN RATHER QUIET IN THE U.K. BY 1905. MOST PEOPLE, INCLUDING THE NEWSPAPERS, WERE NOT PAYING MUCH ATTENTION TO THE WOMEN'S SUFFRAGE CAMPAIGN. BUT THAT WAS ABOUT TO CHANGE.

The British government at the time was Conservative, and their main opposition was the Liberal Party. Campaigning had begun for the 1906 general election, and the Liberals planned a meeting at the Free Trade Hall, Manchester, where MP Sir Edward Grey would speak and then answer questions from the public.

Christabel Pankhurst and fellow WSPU member Annie Kenney decided to go to the meeting. They made a large banner that read WILL THE LIBERAL PARTY GIVE VOTES FOR WOMEN?, which they intended to let down from an upper gallery during the meeting. But they could not get seats in the gallery and had to change their plan at the last moment. They needed something smaller to wave, so they cut down the large banner to just three words: VOTES FOR WOMEN. This slogan would go on to be used around the world.

They waited until a few men had asked questions and been answered before Annie Kenney stood up and asked in a calm voice, "If the Liberal Party is returned to power, will they take steps to give votes to women?"

At the same time, Christabel waved the small VOTES FOR WOMEN banner. There were gasps and shouts of disbelief that a woman would dare to speak out in this way. Annie was forced back into her seat, while a man held his hat over her face to shut her up.

When the rumpus had died down, Christabel shouted out the same question, which again resulted in much heckling from the crowd. In the face of such disorder, the meeting was brought to an abrupt end, but the two women were not about to be ignored. They cried out again and again, "The question! The question! Answer the question!"

The crowd became angry, attacking Christabel and Annie, who were dragged outside and flung onto the street. Passersby stopped to see what all the fuss was about, and Annie and Christabel were arrested for causing an obstruction. Christabel was also charged with assaulting a police officer by spitting in his face after her ejection from the hall.

The two women were given a choice between a fine and a prison sentence. Both chose prison, saying, "We will get our question answered, or sleep in prison tonight."

The WSPU vowed to disrupt all Liberal Party meetings from then on until their question was answered.

1906: Bang, Bang on the Door

THE PRESS REPORTS OF WHAT HAD HAPPENED AT MANCHESTER'S FREE TRADE HALL IN 1905 SPREAD OUTRAGE THROUGHOUT THE U.K.

The arrest of Christabel Pankhurst and Annie Kenney made headlines everywhere. Some people were horrified by the women's behavior; others were horrified by how the authorities had treated them. But their act of civil disobedience energized a new interest in the campaign.

Civil disobedience means deliberately refusing to obey the government. It is a way of protesting against certain laws to draw attention to an issue. After 1905, it became the chief weapon of the WSPU.

As more and more women joined in the heckling and disrupting of political meetings and rallies, the newspapers really started to take notice. There were reports of women being arrested for repeatedly knocking on the door of Number 10 Downing Street, the U.K. government headquarters, for jumping on the prime minister's car, and for chaining themselves to the railings of government buildings and even of Buckingham Palace.

The WSPU was finding new ways of attracting publicity, and Number 10 Downing Street was to become a frequent target throughout the campaign.

In 1909, Daisy Solomon and Elspeth McClelland tried to deliver a message personally to the prime minister by mailing themselves to him. At this time, post office regulations allowed individuals to be "posted," so the two women paid to have themselves delivered to Downing Street by a telegraph messenger boy. The butler who came to the door refused to sign for the "human letters," and eventually they were returned to the offices of the WSPU. But not before the press had taken photographs, ready for the next day's newspapers.

Society was scandalized by such reports: this was not the behavior expected of respectable ladies. But it showed just how determined members of the WSPU were to win. The government continued to ignore these campaigners, dismissing them as hysterical, shrieking women. But they were not about to give up.

Some of the other suffragist societies became annoyed with the WSPU, claiming its militant actions were damaging their own tactics of persistent, law-abiding lobbying of the government.

But it was too late. Civil disobedience was getting gradually more extreme. And the newspapers loved it.

1906: "–ette"

AS THE ACTIONS OF THE WSPU GREW MORE DARING, JOURNALISTS BEGAN TO TAKE MORE INTEREST. ONE OF THESE WAS CHARLES E. HANDS OF THE LONDON *DAILY MAIL*.

In a report on the disruptive behavior of the WSPU in 1906, he changed the word "suffragist" to "suffragette" to distinguish the militant members of the WSPU from the more peaceful, law-abiding members of the other suffrage societies.

There was a fashion to add "–ette" to the ends of words to describe things as small, inferior, or feminine (which, in the eyes of many people at the time, amounted to the same thing). So a small kitchen would be a kitchenette; a short book might be called a novelette; and a cheap substitute for leather made of paper or cloth was called leatherette. Replacing the "–ist" at the end of "suffragist" with "–ette" made the word seem insignificant, small, silly, or fake. Calling the militant members of the WSPU "suffragettes" was a way of making fun of them, like a bully calling you a bad name.

But something strange happened. Instead of being upset or angry about being called suffragettes, the

WSPU members reclaimed the word, proudly using it to describe themselves. They said that "Suffragists 'jist' want the vote, but us Suffragettes intend to 'get' it."

The WSPU recognized that the term *suffragette* would catch the attention of the general public—which is exactly what they wanted. In 1912, they named their second newspaper the *Suffragette* (which changed to *Britannia* at the outbreak of war in 1914).

The word *suffragette* was used only to describe members of the WSPU, who were all women, whereas *suffragist* was used for any woman or man campaigning for votes for women in the U.K., the U.S., and elsewhere in the world.

But although their strategies might differ, both suffragettes and suffragists were equally determined to win their fight for votes for women.

1906: Rotten Fish and Bad Eggs

AT A TIME WITH NO TELEVISION, INTERNET, CELL PHONES, OR EVEN NATIONAL RADIO BROADCASTS, PUBLIC SPEECHES WERE ESSENTIAL IN ORDER TO REACH A LOT OF PEOPLE.

The suffragists and suffragettes in the U.K. and U.S. gave a great many speeches so that people could hear what they were asking for and why they wanted it. The speeches might be made to hundreds of factory workers at the end of their working day, when the speaker had to climb onto a cart or a chair to be seen above the assembled crowds outside the factory gates. Or they might be made to thousands of people at grand gatherings in parks or squares in towns and cities. In London's Trafalgar Square, the speakers stood high on the foundation of one of the famous lion statues. Journalists stood in front of them, writing down what they said in order to print it in the newspapers, so that even more people would hear the message.

Prior to a speech, messages would be chalked on walls and sidewalks to display the names of the speakers and the speech's time, with arrows directing people where to go.

This meant that troublemakers also knew where to go, and they would turn up to disrupt and intimidate the speakers, who were easy targets for abuse. The speakers were sometimes pelted with oranges or worse, or shot at by children with peashooters. Some speakers would wear waterproof coats for protection against the rotten fish and bad eggs that would be hurled their way. They were often jeered at by the angry crowd shouting "Down with suffragettes!" "Go back home and mind the babies!" and even "Throw them in the river!"

But nothing stopped them from speaking. They persisted, so that thousands of women and men got to hear about the fight for equal rights. As a result, many in the audience joined suffrage societies, increasing the membership to create a stronger force ready to stand up to the government.

The campaigns reached all corners of society, from the wealthiest to the poorest, with speakers coming from all classes. Working women, who were often less accustomed to speaking in public than those in the middle or upper classes, were given lessons in public speaking. They were encouraged to give speeches not only to working-class women, who knew all too well the hardships of a working life, but also to middle-class and wealthy women's groups. They told stories from personal experience about life with low pay and poor working conditions, to remind the rich of just how important it was to include *all* women's needs in the demand for equal rights. They were campaigning not only for the vote itself but also for wide social reform in all walks of life.

ANNIE KENNEY (1879–1953)
The only working-class woman to be part of the WSPU hierarchy, she worked in a cotton mill from the age of ten and lost a finger in an accident there. She was imprisoned and force-fed many times.

VERA "JACK" HOLME (1881–1973)
Chauffeur to the WSPU leaders, she was a member of the Actresses' Franchise League, which staged women's suffrage plays. She was an ambulance driver in the First World War.

SYLVIA PANKHURST (1882–1960)
An artist, she designed many of the WSPU's posters and banners. She was imprisoned and force-fed many times. During the First World War, she helped open four mother-and-baby clinics.

MARION WALLACE-DUNLOP (1864–1942)
A sculptor and book illustrator, she was the first suffragette to go on hunger strike when she was imprisoned for throwing stones through the windows of Number 10 Downing Street.

Notable Suffragettes

From princesses to seamstresses, nearly 8,000 women signed up for the WSPU to join the fight for political equality. Some of them resorted to violence to catch the attention of the public, press, and government. More than one thousand went to prison, where hundreds joined the hunger strike and were forcibly fed. They had many slogans and mottoes, one of which was "Make More Noise."

ROSA MAY BILLINGHURST (1875–1953)
Imprisoned and force-fed, she was often seen in her three-wheeled wheelchair at suffragette protests and went on raids to drop ink bombs into mailboxes around London.

EMMELINE PETHICK-LAWRENCE (1867–1954)
Treasurer of the WSPU and coeditor of *Votes for Women*, she created the green, white, and purple color scheme of the WSPU. She was imprisoned and force-fed.

FREDERICK PETHICK-LAWRENCE (1871–1961)
The only man to help with the management of the WSPU, he was the husband of Emmeline. He became an MP in 1923, beating his old enemy, Winston Churchill, in the election.

"GENERAL" FLORA DRUMMOND (1879–1949)
A key organizer for the WSPU's Scottish branch, she later moved to London. She got her nickname by often riding her horse at the front of processions, dressed in a military-style uniform.

JULIA SCURR (1871–1927)
A member of the East London Federation of the
Suffragettes (ELFS), she led a delegation
to the prime minister protesting about
women's low wages in 1914.

EMILY WILDING DAVISON (1872–1913)
Fiercely militant, she was frequently imprisoned and
force-fed. Once, she barricaded herself into her cell,
and the guards filled it with water from a hose
before the door was broken down.

MARY LEIGH (1885–1978)
One of the first to smash windows in protest, she
was involved in many of the most attention-grabbing
suffragette protests. Frequently imprisoned and force-fed,
she was also a drum major in the WSPU band.

UNA DUGDALE (1879–1975)
She caused a scandal by wanting to cut "obey" from her
wedding vows, although she did not when told it would
invalidate her marriage. She later wrote a pamphlet titled
Love and Honour but Not Obey.

EDITH NEW (1877–1951)
A schoolteacher and militant campaigner
for the WSPU, she was one of the first to smash
windows in protest. She was imprisoned and
force-fed many times.

EDITH GARRUD (1872–1971)
A jujitsu instructor, she trained the suffragettes in
self-defense, in particular the bodyguard of thirty
women known as the Amazons whose job it
was to protect the leaders of the WSPU.

PRINCESS SOPHIA DULEEP SINGH (1876–1948)
Although she was a member of the Tax Resistance League
and the WSPU, the authorities refused to send her to
prison because of her royal connections. She went on to
become a nurse in the First World War.

CHRISTABEL PANKHURST (1880–1958)
Emmeline Pankhurst's eldest daughter became
the key strategist for the WSPU and was one of its
most powerful public speakers, with a high profile
in the national press.

LADY CONSTANCE LYTTON (1869–1923)
She exposed the double standards of treatment for
working-class and upper-class prisoners by dressing as
a seamstress and going by the name of Jane Wharton,
in which disguise she was force-fed.

Suffragist

Democratic

Run like a union

NUWSS, NAWSA, and all other suffrage societies

Leaders chosen by members

Peaceful and law-abiding

No slogan

Believed that the violent acts committed by the suffragettes damaged the cause of women's suffrage and hindered support

Included men as members of male suffrage societies and supporters of women's suffrage

Continued throughout the war to protest for women's votes

Maintained peaceful protest throughout the whole campaign

 Campaigning began in mid-1800s

Suffragette

Autocratic

Run like an army

WSPU

Leaders
not elected

Militant, lawbreaking,
ready to commit
civil disobedience

"Deeds, Not Words"

Campaigning
began in 1903

Believed that violent acts
(against property, not
human life) would be
the only way to bring about
change

Did not really want to
have men as members,
since they believed women
should be independent

Ceased all
militant action on
the declaration of
war in 1914

Performed acts of civil
disobedience from
1905 to 1914

1907: Mud, Mud, Mud!

THE WEATHER ON SATURDAY, FEBRUARY 9, 1907, WAS DREADFUL: POURING RAIN, FREEZING COLD, AND FOGGY. THE STREETS IN LONDON WERE HEAVY WITH WET, SPLATTERING MUD.

This was not a day you would expect to find ladies in fine dresses and elegant hats marching through the streets carrying banners proclaiming FAILURE IS IMPOSSIBLE, BE RIGHT AND PERSIST, and JUSTICE, NOT PRIVILEGE. But that was the spectacle thousands of onlookers witnessed that day in London.

It was the first big procession organized by the NUWSS to show the government and the public that, contrary to what they thought, lots of women *did* want the vote.

The Artists' Suffrage League designed posters and postcards advertising the event. Women "of all classes" were urged to "take part in this procession and prove your earnestness in a manner both effective and constitutional."

This was to be a dignified, law-abiding procession. Participants were to assemble at the bandstand at Hyde Park Corner at two in the afternoon and parade to Exeter Hall in the Strand, where various speakers would address a campaign meeting.

More than 3,000 women from over forty suffrage societies turned up in the rain to walk the two-mile route.

Millicent Fawcett, who had helped arrange the march, remarked, "The London weather did its worst against us. Mud, mud, mud was its prominent feature."

But this did not deter the women who came from all over the country and from every class and profession: factory workers, textile workers, and nurses marched alongside artists, writers, and doctors. Upper-class ladies from rich and famous families and ordinary working-class women all came together that day.

The WSPU had not been officially invited because some of the other societies like the Women's Liberal Federation (WLF) and the British Women's Temperance Association (BWTA) did not approve of their militant actions, but some came anyway, and a small group of suffragettes sneaked in to march alongside the others.

What a spectacle it must have been, with the hats, ribbons, and scarves in the NUWSS colors of red and white blowing in the wind amid all that rain and mud.

We are used to seeing people marching in protest against government decisions nowadays, but back in 1907, it would have been unusual and even shocking to see so many women join a protest march. The press loved it and filled their newspapers with reports from the day.

These women were incredibly brave. Some of them worried they might ruin their reputations by being seen in public this way, while others were afraid they might lose their jobs. But they were bringing attention to their cause, which they considered worth the risk.

What became known as the Mud March was considered a tremendous success. Many, many more marches would follow, showing the government and those opposed to women's suffrage that women would stand together, shoulder to shoulder, friend alongside friend, in their struggle to win the vote.

1907: "Dare to Be Free"

WITH SO MANY PEOPLE JOINING THE FIGHT FOR SUFFRAGE, DIFFERENT OPINIONS WERE BOUND TO CAUSE RIFTS EVEN WITHIN LIKE-MINDED GROUPS.

Christabel and Emmeline Pankhurst were both extremely strict leaders; they, along with Emmeline Pethick-Lawrence, made all the major decisions regarding the WSPU. Most members were happy with that arrangement, but any who disagreed with them had no choice but to put up with it or leave.

In 1907, a small group of Christabel and Emmeline's friends challenged them to make the WSPU more democratic. The Pankhursts' answer was a resounding "NO!," so Charlotte Despard, along with seventy other women, broke free from the WSPU to form the Women's Freedom League (WFL).

The WFL's members were mostly pacifists, which meant they were against war or violence of any kind.

Unlike the WSPU, which, like the NUWSS, was focused mainly on winning the vote for women on the same terms as men (which meant for wealthier, middle-class women), the WFL declared they wanted votes for *all* men and women, rich and poor, on equal terms. Like the WSPU, they also wanted to see women get equal pay with men and to receive equal job opportunities. With their motto, "Dare to Be Free," they very soon had thousands of enthusiastic members.

The WFL worked hard. They printed their own newspaper called the *Vote,* which was well written and became a great way for them to criticize the government.

To gain new recruits, they traveled the country in a horse-drawn caravan, stopping in towns and villages to give speeches and sell their newspaper.

They were militant like the WSPU and prepared to break the law, but only in nonviolent ways. They spoke out in court when suffrage campaigners had been arrested, protesting at the trial of women by men under laws made only by men: "Until women are voters, law is but the will of men. It is not human justice."

They even visited members of the government at home in order to state their case, and in 1909, members of the WFL protested peacefully outside the House of Commons for three months, demanding to speak directly to the prime minister, who ignored them.

One hundred WFL members were sent to prison because one of their main weapons of protest was to refuse to pay taxes. Their argument was the same as Mary Smith's had been when she wrote her petition in 1832: Why should women pay tax to a government over which, without a vote, they had no influence at all? Their campaign of "No taxation without representation" was a practical and effective tool against government.

1907: Votes for Women? Never!

"THE CAT, THE WOMAN, AND THE CHIMNEY SHOULD NEVER LEAVE THE HOUSE." THIS OLD SAYING NOW SEEMS SHOCKING, BUT IT SUMS UP HOW MANY PEOPLE IN BRITAIN STILL FELT AT THE TURN OF THE TWENTIETH CENTURY.

The very thought of giving women the parliamentary vote was exceedingly unpopular—among both men and women. Women were seen by many as physically, emotionally, and intellectually inferior to men. How could they possibly be trusted to cast a vote?

As the suffragist campaign grew and spoke with a louder, stronger voice, the people who were opposed to women voting spoke up too. They became known as the National League for Opposing Woman Suffrage, or the "Antis," and they all had a good laugh at the men and women who were campaigning for change. Some people don't like change because it makes them nervous, and the Antis were very nervous about what the country, even the world, would look like if women were making important political decisions.

The Antis made all sorts of extraordinary claims as to why women should not be allowed to vote: They said women were ruled by impulse and emotion and could never think logically; that women's minds were full of childish thoughts, like what hat to wear, what pretty dress to buy, which dreamy man to marry, gossip, chocolate, babies, puppies, and kittens. They said women were irrational, fickle, and unable to make reasonable judgments. They should stay at home, sewing, doing embroidery, and drinking tea. One MP remarked, "Votes for women? What shall we be asked next? To give votes to our horses and dogs?"

The Antis placed advertisements in newspapers and magazines and printed postcards and posters to undermine the campaign for votes for women. Some even ridiculed protesting women by pinning insulting labels on their backs.

But it would be wrong to assume that these ideas came only from men exerting their presumed superiority over women. Some of the most outspoken opponents to women's suffrage were women themselves, who said they were perfectly happy to let their menfolk make decisions on their behalf. They believed that if they gained the vote on equal terms with men, it would bring about an end to family life, even an end to civilization itself. At a time when the likelihood of war felt very real, there was also a fear, among both men and women, that if women voted, the country would embrace pacifism, resulting in men refusing to fight in a war to defend the country.

In any case, many believed that the majority of women didn't even want the vote.

Notable British Antis

T HE NATIONAL LEAGUE FOR OPPOSING WOMEN'S SUFFRAGE WAS FORMED WHEN THE WOMEN'S NATIONAL ANTI-SUFFRAGE LEAGUE JOINED WITH THE MEN'S LEAGUE FOR OPPOSING WOMAN SUFFRAGE IN 1910.

At its peak in 1914, there were 42,000 members, only one in five of which were men. It is surprising that so many women were opposed to their own enfranchisement, but they clearly felt they had the support of the public when more than 300,000 people signed a petition against votes for women.

Some of the strongest Antis were also social reformers and avid campaigners for improving the education and living standards for the poor, especially for women. And yet they held an unflinching belief that women should be kept well away from the complexities of politics.

While many remained firmly against women's suffrage, some changed their minds in time and went on to support it.

GERTRUDE BELL (1868–1926)
An archaeologist and explorer, she traveled all over the world and even established the Iraq Museum in Baghdad, an extraordinary achievement. Strangely, she was also one of the leaders of the Anti-Suffrage League, believing that most women lacked the education needed to understand politics, and therefore a vote would be wasted on them.

LORD CURZON (1859–1925)
Viceroy of India and later foreign secretary, he was an opponent of women's suffrage and in 1910 appealed for support in the *Times* newspaper. One man replied, "More men than you perhaps guess have nothing but pity left for the rubbish you talk." Undaunted, Lord Curzon became president of the National League for Opposing Woman Suffrage in 1912.

QUEEN VICTORIA (1819–1901)
During her sixty-three-year reign (1837–1901), she was one of the most powerful leaders in the world yet remained fiercely opposed to "Women's Rights," which she once called "a wicked folly." One of her daughters, Princess Louise, met with suffragists in private but could not offer support in public because of her mother's views.

ETHEL BERTHA HARRISON (1851–1916)
A wealthy society lady educated by French and English governesses, she was one of the leaders of the Women's National Anti-Suffrage League and wrote anti-suffrage essays, expressing her opinion that women were by nature unsuited to political activities. She also wrote and published a series of hymns.

MRS. HUMPHRY WARD (1851–1920)
Using her married name, she was a successful novelist and a founder of the Women's Anti-Suffrage League. The writer Virginia Woolf (a supporter of women's suffrage) said after her death, "Mrs. Ward is dead; poor Mrs. Humphry Ward; and it appears that she was merely a woman of straw after all—shoveled into the ground and already forgotten."

LADY JERSEY (1849–1945)
Lady Jersey was one of several members of the aristocracy involved in the formation of the Women's National Anti-Suffrage League and chaired their first meeting, held on July 21, 1908, at the Westminster Palace Hotel in London. She believed that to give women the vote in parliamentary elections would prove little short of a disaster.

HERBERT HENRY (HH) ASQUITH (1852–1928)
As prime minister from 1908 to 1916, he was considered by the suffragettes to be their bitterest enemy. He dashed their hopes whenever it looked as if a law might be passed to give women the vote. At the same time, he did introduce radical laws to provide pensions for the elderly and financial support for the unemployed, disabled, and ill.

WINSTON CHURCHILL (1874–1965)
As home secretary, he was responsible for repressing the militant activism of the suffragettes, who blamed him for the atrocities of Black Friday (see page 76). He claimed women did not need the vote because they were "well represented by their fathers, brothers, and husbands," but later changed his mind and voted in favor of limited women's suffrage in 1918.

VIOLET MARKHAM (1872–1959)
She worked to improve the lives of the poor and the unemployed all her life but was also an avid supporter of the Women's Anti-Suffrage League. Having campaigned hard against women getting the vote, speaking out at major venues including the Albert Hall in London, she herself ran for Parliament in the general election of 1918. She lost, but later became mayor of Chesterfield.

THE DUCHESS OF MONTROSE (1854–1940)
President of the Scottish National Anti-Suffrage League, she believed women were incapable of making political decisions. And yet she used her own wealth and position in society to support many good causes, from the training of midwives and nurses to vacation homes for children in poverty. She was also president of the Scottish Red Cross.

1908: Breaking Glass

THE SUFFRAGETTES' MOTTO OF "DEEDS, NOT WORDS" WAS WORKING, AND ACTS OF CIVIL DISOBEDIENCE BY MEMBERS OF THE WSPU WERE BECOMING MUCH MORE FREQUENT.

Now the sound of women heckling politicians was joined by a new sound that reached the very heart of the government: the sound of breaking glass. It would prove to be a very powerful noise.

On June 30, 1908, two suffragettes, Mary Leigh and Edith New, went to Downing Street armed with stones. When they arrived at Number 10, the U.K. government headquarters, they flung the stones at the windows, smashing and shattering the glass. Of course, they were both arrested and sent to Holloway Prison for two months.

This wasn't their first act of civil disobedience. Edith had previously been arrested for chaining herself to the railings at 10 Downing Street, and Mary had been sent to prison in 1907 when a suffragette march to Parliament turned violent.

It was, however, seen as the first act of vandalism by suffragettes. Over the coming years, hundreds of windows would be smashed, causing thousands of British pounds' worth of damage, in the fight to win the vote.

On their release from jail, Mary and Edith were treated as heroines by their fellow suffragettes, who met them at the prison gates and took them to a celebratory breakfast held in their honor. They traveled in an open carriage drawn not by horses but by a team of suffragettes, accompanied by rousing brass bands.

Rather than apologize for their violent actions, they made this threat: If women don't get the vote, "It will be bombs next time!"

1908: Prime Enemy

THE SUFFRAGETTES KNEW THEY WERE FIGHTING A WAR. THEY HAD MANY ENEMIES, BUT PERHAPS THEIR MOST BOTHERSOME, UNYIELDING FOE WAS THE BRITISH PRIME MINISTER HIMSELF.

Herbert Henry Asquith, known as HH for short, became the leader of the Liberal Party and prime minister of the U.K. in April 1908. This was not good news for the suffragettes: HH was firmly set against giving women the vote. Many Liberal MPs did support votes for women, but Mr. Asquith just didn't take the idea of women voters seriously. He refused to believe that the public supported women's suffrage and demanded proof that society would be better if women had the vote or, indeed, that most women even wanted the vote.

The suffragists answered him by holding a huge rally in London's Hyde Park in 1908 with well over 250,000—some say even half a million—people, all chanting, "Votes for women!"

But still he would not listen, and he repeatedly refused to meet with leaders of the various women's suffrage societies, in particular the WSPU.

The suffragettes were getting on his nerves. He was their main target, and they attacked him whenever they could get close enough. He was jeered at, slapped, and even whipped. On one occasion, a pleasant game of golf in Scotland was ruined when two suffragettes got on the course and harangued him. (Mr. Asquith was particularly vexed about that.)

They jumped on his car, smashed his windows, and chained themselves to his railings. In Birmingham, England, they threw roof slates at him. In Dublin, Ireland, they tried to burn down the theater where he was due to give a speech, and on the same visit, Mary Leigh even hurled an ax at the carriage in which he was traveling. Luckily it missed, but it did cut the ear of the MP he was with, John Redmond.

All this did nothing to change the prime minister's mind. In fact, it only made him more stubborn.

Eventually he did agree to meet with the more peaceful, non-ax-wielding Millicent Fawcett and a small group from the NUWSS. But no matter what they said, he wouldn't budge. Over the years of his prime ministership, Mr. Asquith remained steadfastly opposed to women voters, and so the war between the suffragettes and the prime minister raged on.

1908: The Trojan Horse Raid

SUFFRAGETTES WERE FREQUENTLY STOPPED FROM ENTERING PARLIAMENT BUILDINGS. HECKLING, BOOING, EVEN PHYSICAL ATTACKS ON MEMBERS OF PARLIAMENT HAD WORN THE PATIENCE OF THE GOVERNMENT PAPER-THIN.

The government was so nervous that Parliament was occasionally surrounded by an army of policemen to stop the women from getting in.

But suffragettes didn't give up so easily, especially Christabel Pankhurst, who thought up a new tactic. When a big furniture truck trundled up to the gates one day in 1908, the police thought nothing of it and let it pass through.

As soon as the truck was inside, more than twenty suffragettes leaped from the back and made a dash for the entrance to the building. The startled police gave chase and grabbed all but two, who barged straight into Parliament, shouting "Votes for women!"

The newspapers thought this was hilarious and called it the Trojan Horse Raid. The story of how the suffragettes outwitted the police was reported as far away as New Zealand, where the *Auckland Star* commented, "Such determination and pluck must surely win in the end."

There was still a long way to go, but through such exploits, the campaign for votes for women was getting noticed.

The Rebel Princess

SOPHIA DULEEP SINGH WAS A SUFFRAGETTE, A POLITICAL REBEL, AND . . . A PRINCESS.

Her grandfather was the Great Maharaja Ranjit Singh, who was so powerful that he was nicknamed the Lion of the Punjab. But when he died, his son, Duleep Singh, Sophia's father, was only a child, and the British, who at the time ruled India, forced him to sign away all his inheritance.

At the age of fifteen, Duleep was exiled from India to England, where he became a favorite of Queen Victoria. When his daughter, Princess Sophia, was born in 1876, Queen Victoria became her godmother.

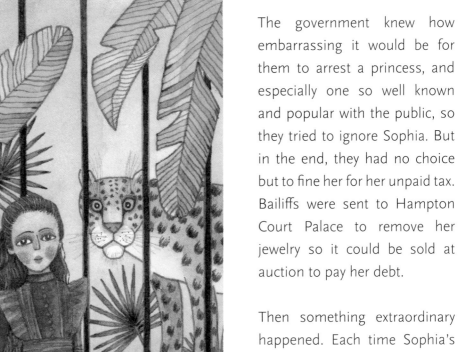

Princess Sophia grew up in high society, mingling with aristocrats and royalty. As a child, she had cheetahs and leopards as pets, and as she grew up, her face was in all the magazines, just like a celebrity of today.

But Princess Sophia was troubled by how her family had been cheated by the British, and came to realize she needed more than fancy clothes and parties to fill her life.

Then, in 1908, she met Una Dugdale, a suffragette who told Sophia exciting stories about the WSPU. They captured Sophia's imagination and she decided to dedicate herself to the fight for women's rights.

Sophia would regularly sell the newspaper the *Suffragette* outside her home, Hampton Court Palace. It was brilliant publicity for the campaign. She also joined the Women's Tax Resistance League, whose members refused to pay any tax until women were given the right to vote: "No vote, no tax."

The government knew how embarrassing it would be for them to arrest a princess, and especially one so well known and popular with the public, so they tried to ignore Sophia. But in the end, they had no choice but to fine her for her unpaid tax. Bailiffs were sent to Hampton Court Palace to remove her jewelry so it could be sold at auction to pay her debt.

Then something extraordinary happened. Each time Sophia's jewelry was to be sold, the auction house would fill with rich ladies, but no one would bid. Instead of the price going up, it would go down, until just one lady would bid, buying the jewelry for a pittance. Next, in a show of sheer defiance to the authorities, whoever had bought the jewelry would make a big display of handing it back to Princess Sophia, who always just happened to be in the audience.

The suffragettes were still finding new ways to defy the government and bring attention to their campaign.

1909: Hunger Strike

PRISON IN BRITAIN IN THE EARLY TWENTIETH CENTURY WAS HORRIBLE; MUCH WORSE THAN IT IS TODAY. DRAFTY AND COLD IN WINTER, HOT AND MUGGY IN SUMMER, STINKY ALL YEAR ROUND; DIMLY LIT AND GRIM, WITH HARD PRISON BEDS THAT WERE NO MORE THAN PLANKS OF WOOD, AND ICE-COLD WATER TO WASH IN: PRISON WAS A PLACE TO BE AVOIDED AT ALL COSTS.

So even if you disagree with the illegal antics of the militant suffragettes, it is hard not to acknowledge the incredible bravery and courage it took for them to knowingly break the law, understanding as they did that they would be sent to jail.

Most judges offered them a choice of a fine or a prison sentence, but most suffragettes chose prison.

Of course this scandalized and shocked the public. But the suffragettes recognized value in attracting attention and sympathy for their cause, especially the sight of refined, educated, respectable ladies being treated so brutally by the authorities.

At the time, prisoners were separated into three divisions. The third division was for ordinary criminals, whose sentences were often accompanied by "hard labor," meaning they were given tough physical tasks to perform as part of their punishment.

The second division was for prisoners considered to be of better character, or who were being imprisoned for more minor offenses such as refusing to pay a fine. These prisoners had to spend the first four weeks of their sentence in solitary confinement, unable to speak to anyone. During their time in prison, they were allowed no books and almost no visitors. They were not even allowed to send or receive letters and so had no news from home or about what was happening in the outside world.

Meanwhile, first-division prisoners had newspapers as well as books and were allowed to correspond with their friends and family and have frequent visits from them. They wore their own clothes and were even allowed to send out for their own food. Political prisoners were classed as first division.

On entering prison, the suffragettes always demanded to be allowed this special treatment given to

A badge was cheap and could be pinned to a coat or jacket or dress and worn with pride, declaring to everyone that its wearer was a supporter of votes for women. Badges were popular in both the U.K. and the U.S. Lots of suffrage groups made badges, usually in the colors of each group.

Of course, the opposing side had badges too. The Women's National Anti-Suffrage League and the National League for Opposing Woman Suffrage both decorated their badges with a rose, a thistle, and a clover, representing England, Scotland, and Ireland, as a united force saying a very firm "NO" to votes for women.

1909: Hunger Strike

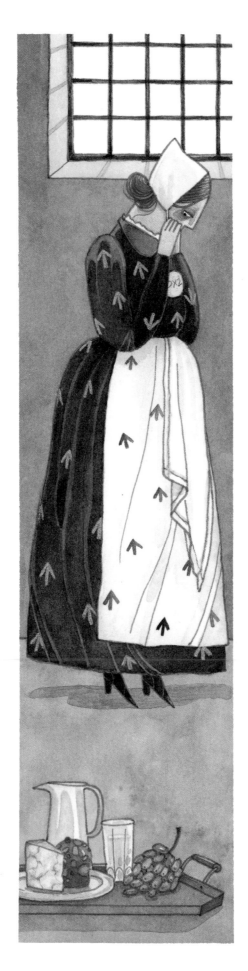

PRISON IN BRITAIN IN THE EARLY TWENTIETH CENTURY WAS HORRIBLE; MUCH WORSE THAN IT IS TODAY. DRAFTY AND COLD IN WINTER, HOT AND MUGGY IN SUMMER, STINKY ALL YEAR ROUND; DIMLY LIT AND GRIM, WITH HARD PRISON BEDS THAT WERE NO MORE THAN PLANKS OF WOOD, AND ICE-COLD WATER TO WASH IN: PRISON WAS A PLACE TO BE AVOIDED AT ALL COSTS.

So even if you disagree with the illegal antics of the militant suffragettes, it is hard not to acknowledge the incredible bravery and courage it took for them to knowingly break the law, understanding as they did that they would be sent to jail.

Most judges offered them a choice of a fine or a prison sentence, but most suffragettes chose prison.

Of course this scandalized and shocked the public. But the suffragettes recognized value in attracting attention and sympathy for their cause, especially the sight of refined, educated, respectable ladies being treated so brutally by the authorities.

At the time, prisoners were separated into three divisions. The third division was for ordinary criminals, whose sentences were often accompanied by "hard labor," meaning they were given tough physical tasks to perform as part of their punishment.

The second division was for prisoners considered to be of better character, or who were being imprisoned for more minor offenses such as refusing to pay a fine. These prisoners had to spend the first four weeks of their sentence in solitary confinement, unable to speak to anyone. During their time in prison, they were allowed no books and almost no visitors. They were not even allowed to send or receive letters and so had no news from home or about what was happening in the outside world.

Meanwhile, first-division prisoners had newspapers as well as books and were allowed to correspond with their friends and family and have frequent visits from them. They wore their own clothes and were even allowed to send out for their own food. Political prisoners were classed as first division.

On entering prison, the suffragettes always demanded to be allowed this special treatment given to

Pins and Badges

A BADGE IS AN INGENIOUS THING. IT IS SO SIMPLE, AND WEARING ONE IS SUCH AN EASY WAY TO SHOW YOU SUPPORT SOMETHING.

Some supporters of votes for women were very poor. They couldn't afford to dress up in the colors of the WSPU: for instance, purple hats or skirts, green dresses or jackets, white gloves. In fact, they might have owned only one dress, and that was probably gray or brown or black.

political prisoners—after all, they were fighting the government on a political point. But the authorities would have none of that. They treated the suffragettes just the same as any ordinary criminals, usually as second-division, but sometimes even as third-division prisoners.

The suffragettes had to wear prison uniforms: white cap, rough black dress covered in white arrows, white cotton apron covered with black arrows, itchy red-and-brown-striped stockings, and run-down old shoes that were probably full of holes. Big round leather labels were pinned to their clothes and printed with their cell numbers.

No letters or visitors; no books or newspapers. There was only hard work and horrid, bland prison food.

In 1909, at Holloway Prison in London, one prisoner had an idea about how she could continue her protest to win votes for women while being locked up. She went on hunger strike.

The prisoner's name was Marion Wallace-Dunlop. She was an artist, serving a month-long prison sentence for graffiti in the House of Commons, where she had printed a protest message on a wall with a rubber stamp.

Three days into her sentence, Marion refused to eat anything. For several days, the prison authorities tried to tempt her to eat by replacing the normal poor, boring prison food with delicious meals that would be left all day long in her cell to torment her. But Marion wouldn't eat a crumb.

There was a real fear that she might starve herself to death, so after ninety-one hours on hunger strike, Marion was released from prison.

Hunger strike was no fun at all. The pain and misery of hunger would cause depression, stomach pain, headache, dizziness, and exhaustion. But Marion had started something that would inspire hundreds more suffragette prisoners to do the same.

It caused consternation for the prison authorities. They didn't know what to do, except to release the hunger strikers from their prison sentences early, when they became so weak that it looked as if they might actually die. The authorities were losing control of the situation.

But it didn't take long before a royal voice spoke up with a menacing suggestion. The king himself wondered why on earth these women were not being forcibly fed.

1909: The Gag, the Tube, and the Funnel

TO BE FORCE-FED WAS TORTURE, A HORROR SUFFRAGETTES LIKE ELSIE DUVAL AND HUGH FRANKLIN KNEW ONLY TOO WELL.

The prisoner was held, or even tied, to a bed or chair by the prison wardens. Then a painful metal gag would be pushed into the prisoner's mouth to pry it open, and a rubber tube forced down the throat. If that failed, the tube was shoved up the nose instead. Then a sloppy gloop of eggy, milky, bready goo was poured through a funnel down the tube, directly into the stomach.

Hundreds of suffragettes and their supporters, both women and men, were force-fed. They described the unbearable pain in the nose and throat and chest, the pounding in the head and heart that felt like being choked. Sometimes in the struggle, the sloppy gloop would end up in the prisoners' lungs, leaving them gravely ill. Often they just threw it all back up.

One famous case was that of Lady Constance Lytton. She was arrested during a WSPU protest at the House of Commons, was sent to prison, and went on hunger strike. But unlike working-class prisoners, she was seen by a doctor and released early, without being forcibly fed. Lady Constance became suspicious that she was being treated differently because of who she was. So she cut her hair, put on a shabby dress, and disguised herself as a poor seamstress.

In this disguise, she was arrested while protesting in Liverpool, sent to prison, and again went on hunger strike. This time, because the authorities thought she was a "nobody," no doctor checked her health, and she was forcibly fed. Eventually her real identity was discovered, upon which she was immediately released, but she never quite recovered from the ordeal, and some historians believe it contributed to her early death.

Force-feeding of suffragette prisoners soon became very unpopular with the public. Many MPs were disgusted that the government had agreed to it, one calling it a "beastly outrage," and 116 doctors signed a petition against it. The government didn't know what to do. Some options discussed in Parliament at the time included carting the hunger strikers off to lunatic asylums, shipping them overseas, or even just letting them die.

Giving women the vote was also mentioned, but only as a joke: the government was not about to do that. So they did nothing, and the hunger strikes—and the force-feeding—continued.

1909: The Magnificent Muriel Matters in Her Flying Machine

MURIEL MATTERS WAS TRULY MAGNIFICENT. AN ACTOR, MUSICIAN, AND LATER A VERY TALENTED JOURNALIST, SHE FOUND IMAGINATIVE WAYS TO GAIN ATTENTION FOR THE CAUSE OF VOTES FOR WOMEN.

Muriel was an Australian who moved to the U.K. in 1905. Two years later, she joined the Women's Freedom League (WFL), whose members believed in nonviolent action and protest.

In October 1908, Muriel chained herself to a metal barrier in the Ladies' Gallery at the House of Commons that separated women from men, since in fact it obstructed women's view of Parliament below. She attached herself so well that the whole barrier had to be removed with Muriel still attached to it, while a blacksmith was sent for to cut her free.

But her most daring deed came a year later.

Her friend Henry Spencer had built an eighty-foot hydrogen-filled airship, which gave Muriel an idea. On February 16, 1909, King Edward VII was due to lead a procession for the State Opening of Parliament. What if an airship were to fly overhead, raining down "Votes for Women" leaflets on the king, the procession, the Houses of Parliament, and the crowds below?

The airship was painted on one side with VOTES FOR WOMEN and on the other with THE WOMEN'S FREEDOM LEAGUE, all in huge letters so the words could be read for miles around. On the appointed day, the basket was loaded up with leaflets, and the intrepid Muriel climbed in, followed by Henry. Up, up, up they rose, to a height of 3,500 feet.

It was extremely cold up there in the sky, high above London. To keep warm, Muriel busied herself with throwing out leaflets. She watched nervously as Henry climbed out of the basket and clambered across the delicate frame to make adjustments to the rigging. He made her think of a spider creeping across its web. Suddenly she realized that if Henry fell off, she had no idea how to fly the airship. But she tried not to think about that and continued "making a trail of leaflets across London."

Unfortunately, it was a blustery day, so the airship was blown off course and never made it to the sky above the king's procession. Nonetheless, Muriel flew over the outskirts of London for more than an hour, dropping leaflets onto the streets below . . . before crash-landing into a tree in Coulsdon, a town south of London.

Despite things not going entirely to plan, the flight was declared a great success, and the story of the valiant Muriel Matters and her airship was featured in newspapers around the world.

Pageants and Parades

BRITISH SUFFRAGISTS AND SUFFRAGETTES KNEW HOW TO PUT ON A GOOD SHOW.

All those years spent learning "women's work" came in handy. Crafts that women had been doing since they were little girls were put to great use as they embroidered banners and flags, painted posters, designed badges and jewelry, and knitted scarves.

They wrote poems, performed plays, and organized spectacular parades, all with the intention of showing the public and the government the importance of women's achievements, past and present.

They would often parade dressed up as great women from history. The fifteenth-century French heroine Joan of Arc on horseback was a favorite, representing female rebellion. Others dressed as the novelist Emily Brontë, Queen Boadicea, or Queen Elizabeth I, representing wisdom, strength, and power, respectively.

Different groups of women would march together. For example, some parades were held to celebrate women at work, featuring such professions as nurses, midwives, actresses, journalists, and teachers. Or women from England, Ireland, Scotland, and Wales might join forces and march in the thousands, often wearing traditional or national dress, while Indian women would parade together wearing saris.

Women who had been to jail wanted everyone to know and would make replica costumes of prison uniforms covered in arrows or proudly carry a pole with an arrow at the top.

The atmosphere was always jubilant. Marching bands would play cheery songs, and the women would sing along. In fact, the songs were so catchy that the crowds of spectators would often join in too.

These pageants and parades were a real spectacle, all designed to draw attention to the cause of votes for women.

But was the government listening?

A Riot of Color

LOOKING AT PHOTOGRAPHS OF SUFFRAGISTS ON MARCHES AND CAMPAIGNS, WE SEE A WORLD IN BLACK AND WHITE, BUT IN REALITY IT WOULD HAVE BEEN A RIOT OF COLOR.

All the women's suffrage organizations had banners and flags in their own particular color scheme. Sometimes the colors had meanings.

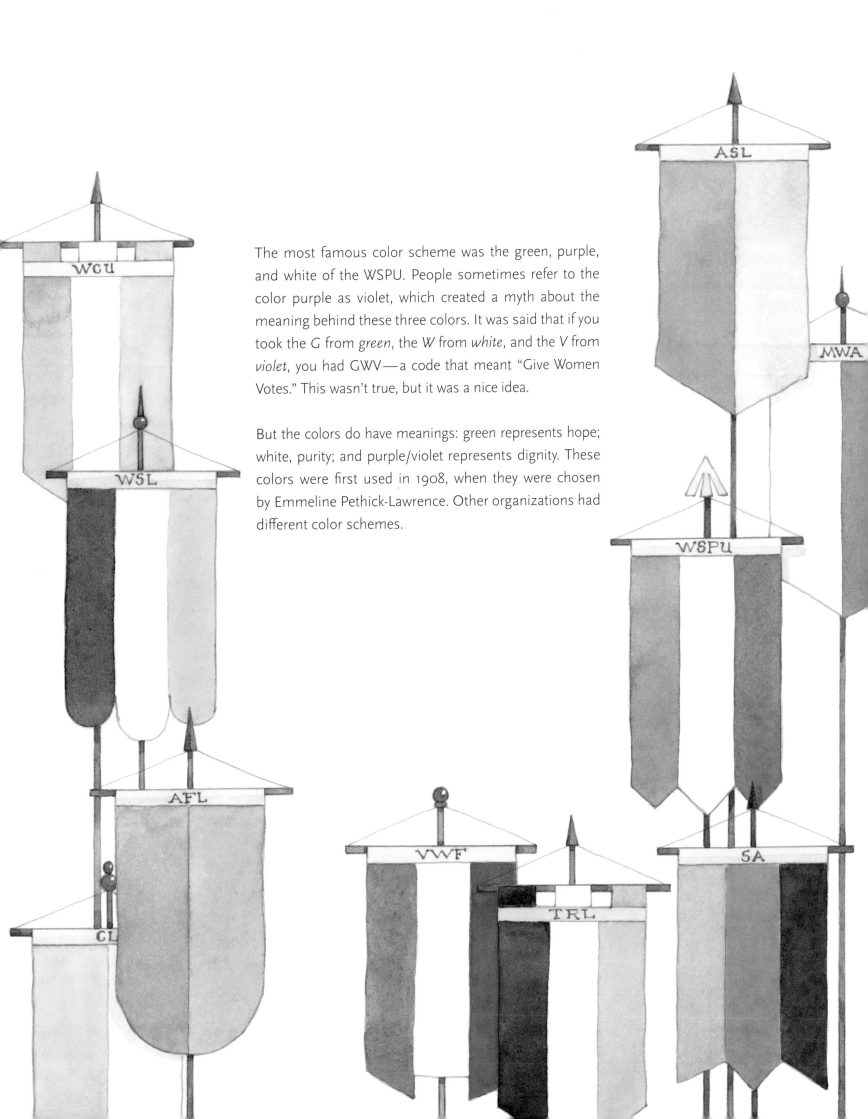

The most famous color scheme was the green, purple, and white of the WSPU. People sometimes refer to the color purple as violet, which created a myth about the meaning behind these three colors. It was said that if you took the G from *green*, the W from *white*, and the V from *violet*, you had GWV—a code that meant "Give Women Votes." This wasn't true, but it was a nice idea.

But the colors do have meanings: green represents hope; white, purity; and purple/violet represents dignity. These colors were first used in 1908, when they were chosen by Emmeline Pethick-Lawrence. Other organizations had different color schemes.

Justice, Liberty, Peace, and Hope

SUFFRAGE CAMPAIGNERS IN BRITAIN AND THE UNITED STATES WERE INTERESTED IN LEARNING FROM ONE ANOTHER, AND OFTEN PROMINENT SUFFRAGISTS FROM EACH COUNTRY WOULD TRAVEL ACROSS THE ATLANTIC OCEAN ON LECTURE TOURS.

One such person was Ida B. Wells-Barnett, who traveled to Britain from her home in Chicago twice. A journalist and a civil rights activist, Ida made the fight against racism and violence toward African Americans her life's work. In reporting on the practice of lynching, in which black men and boys were tortured and hanged for slight or even dubious crimes, she brought national attention and condemnation to this horrific means of intimidating black communities. In 1884, at the age of twenty-two, she sued a train company when she was forcibly removed from a first-class seat in the ladies' carriage by employees who insisted the section was for whites only. She later became an active campaigner for women's suffrage as well.

She knew the fights against racial and gender discrimination couldn't be won without the active political involvement of women, so in 1913 she and fellow suffragist Belle Squire founded the Alpha Suffrage Club, which became the largest and most influential African American women's suffrage association at that time. Her insistence on racial as well as gender equality created discord with some of the organizers of the mainly white suffrage groups.

The National American Woman Suffrage Association planned a parade to take place in Washington, DC, on March 3, 1913. The parade was organized by Alice Paul and intended to upstage the inauguration of President Woodrow Wilson, which was scheduled for the following day. The suffragists knew that national attention would be focused on the capital city for this important event. They thought that if they could capture the attention of the gathered press instead, they could pressure Wilson to take up the cause.

Parades were a big part of the British women's suffrage movement, but a procession on this scale had not yet been part of the American effort. Five thousand suffragists from across the country met that day to march up Pennsylvania Avenue. There were floats, bands, mounted brigades, and women dressed as Justice, Liberty, Peace, and Hope. The entire procession was led by lawyer Inez Milholland, another one of the parade organizers, who was dressed in a flowing white dress and riding a white horse.

But when members of the Chicago Alpha Suffrage Club arrived, they were told that the march was for white suffrage groups only. African Americans would only be permitted to march separately at the back of the parade. Ida B. Wells-Barnett, however, refused to be relegated to the back. Instead she stood among the spectators and waited for the march to begin. When the procession marched past her, she stepped out into the parade to march at the front alongside the white suffragists.

1910–1912: The Bill, the Whole Bill, and Nothing but the Bill

A BILL DESIGNED TO GIVE WOMEN THE VOTE WAS WRITTEN AND READ IN PARLIAMENT EVERY YEAR FROM 1900.

A bill is a draft of a new law or a change to an existing law that is read and discussed by lawmakers, in this case, MPs in Parliament. MPs can then decide if they like the idea or not and so vote for (or against) the bill to create (or prevent) an act of Parliament, which will bring about a new law.

At first Parliament didn't take the idea of giving women the vote seriously at all, and any bill on the subject would be laughed at, abandoned, or "talked out," which meant that MPs just kept talking about any other topic (for example, in 1904, the effectiveness of taillights on what was then a brand-new invention: the motor car). The idea was to keep talking until the time ran out and they all went home, not having even discussed women's votes, let alone passed the bill to make it law.

The suffragists and suffragettes were exasperated each time their bill was dropped, ignored, or rejected. By 1908, most MPs did support giving women the vote, although they could not agree on exactly *which* women: only those who owned property, or a wider group including working-class women?

In 1910 something called a Conciliation Bill was written. The idea was to find a compromise on the subject of women's votes, to "conciliate," or pacify, those who thought it an important issue. Instead of asking for the law to change to allow all women to vote, this Conciliation Bill proposed votes for only the richest and most well-educated women. MPs who supported women's suffrage thought this might be the best offer they could get and so would vote in favor of it.

Others, though, felt their consciences would not allow them to vote for a law that wouldn't include votes for all women, particularly women of the working class, and so they voted against it. Some political parties worried that these one million women who would be given a vote would all vote for the Conservatives and that their own political party would lose power as a result, so they voted against it too. And many Irish MPs voted against it because they were having their own problems in Ireland and wanted the government to focus on that.

But the biggest block to these bills being passed was, once again, Prime Minister Asquith. In all, three separate Conciliation Bills were written, in 1910, 1911, and 1912, but none resulted in a law giving women the vote. The failure of the first bill in 1910 in particular was to have devastating consequences.

1910: Black Friday

HOPES WERE HIGH IN EARLY 1910. IT LOOKED AS IF THE BRITISH GOVERNMENT WAS LISTENING AND MIGHT FINALLY AGREE TO GIVE AT LEAST SOME WOMEN THE VOTE.

A Conciliation Bill was written. If a majority of MPs approved this bill in Parliament, it would change the law to allow just over one million wealthy, property-owning women the vote. This wasn't ideal, as it completely ignored all working-class women and many middle-class women too, but both Millicent Fawcett and Emmeline Pankhurst agreed it was better than nothing and a step in the right direction to one day achieving full suffrage for all women.

A truce was called between the WSPU and the government, and all militant action was stopped. The long, hard battle to win women the vote could soon be over: no more protests, no more prison, no more hunger strikes or force-feeding. Promises had been made, and victory was within reach. Then, right at the last moment, Prime Minister Asquith decided that the Conciliation Bill should be abandoned. The suffragists were right back where they started—with nothing.

All supporters of women's suffrage were extremely upset, but the suffragettes were furious. They felt betrayed by the prime minister and decided that on Friday, November 18, 1910, they would march on Parliament in protest and demand to speak with him.

They knew that if they all marched together, they would be arrested immediately, so they agreed to travel in small groups in order to evade the authorities. Everyone knew that the protest was planned, but there was nothing to be done about just a few women walking through the streets together.

Having gathered in Caxton Hall, three hundred suffragettes set off in groups of twelve at five-minute intervals on the short march to Parliament. Emmeline Pankhurst led the first group, alongside Princess Sophia Duleep Singh; Elizabeth Garrett Anderson (the U.K.'s first female doctor, who was by then seventy-four years old); her daughter, Louise Garrett Anderson (also a doctor); Hertha Ayrton (an engineer, mathematician, and physicist); Dorinda Neligan (a headmistress); and Georgina Solomon (a campaigner for racial and religious equality). Following behind on horseback was Evelina Haverfield, to provide some protection for the women on the ground.

Winston Churchill was then home secretary, which made him responsible for keeping law and order. The last thing he wanted was a crowd of suffragettes ending up in prison and going on hunger strike, with all the bad publicity that would ensue. So in anticipation of the protest (although he later denied it), Churchill gave instructions to the police to keep the women away from Parliament and the prime minister—but not to make any arrests.

This was a recipe for disaster. Crowds had gathered in Westminster on that Friday, curious to see what might happen. As they approached Parliament Square, Mrs. Pankhurst and her leading group were jostled and bumped, but managed to push their way through the crowds to the St. Stephen's entrance of the House of Commons. But as they demanded to speak with Mr. Asquith, the scene behind them turned nasty.

The following groups of suffragettes, blocked by an army of police (some say as many as 5,000), pushed forward again and again but could not break through to join Mrs. Pankhurst and the leading group.

Behind them, the crowd jeered at the women, calling out insults. Some grabbed and snatched their banners, which read THE BILL, THE WHOLE BILL, AND NOTHING BUT THE BILL, and tore them up, laughing and joking with one another.

Determined that the rest of the suffragettes should not be allowed to join Mrs. Pankhurst, the police began breaking up the ever-increasing number arriving in Parliament Square as if they were breaking up a drunken brawl.

The women found themselves being tossed around like rag dolls, pushed violently and repeatedly back and forth from one policeman to another. Punched, battered, kicked, and beaten, some were picked up and flung into the crowds of surrounding men, while others were thrown to the ground, dragged down alleys, and roughed up.

Helpless, Mrs. Pankhurst and her group of mostly elderly ladies watched in horror, screaming for the violence to stop, but the fight raged on for six long hours.

Some police had their helmets knocked off in the frenzy as women were trampled by horses and, in one case, pushed in front of a moving car. Evelina Haverfield charged full speed into the battle, striking policemen's faces with her whip before she was dragged from her horse.

Princess Sophia watched in disbelief as a policeman grabbed a suffragette around her waist and threw her to the ground over and over until she was too weak and dazed to fight back. Sophia ran to the woman's defense, demanding to know the officer's number so she could report him, which she did. But no charges were ever brought against him or against any of the other policemen who acted with such brutality that day.

Eventually the police began arresting people, and more than a hundred women and four men were taken to Bow Street police station in London. All were released without charge the very next day.

The events of November 18 proved to be a disaster for the government. Many people blamed Winston Churchill, and in the days that followed, more than a hundred women made official complaints. They described horrible injuries, telling of arms being twisted and thumbs bent back, of punches to the neck and face, and even of having their skirts lifted up above their heads, which would have been particularly humiliating and shocking.

Later, the violence the suffragettes experienced that day was often cited as justification for the more extreme forms of protest adopted in 1912. What was the point of women being hurt when damage to property drew just as much attention to their cause?

The press sided with the suffragettes, and the *Daily Mirror* printed a photograph on its front page of suffragette Ada Wright lying collapsed on the ground. Highly embarrassed, the government tried to stop the paper from printing the picture, but it was too late. The story of Black Friday, as it became known, was there for the world to see. If the government had hoped to suppress the suffragettes' protest, it had achieved the exact opposite.

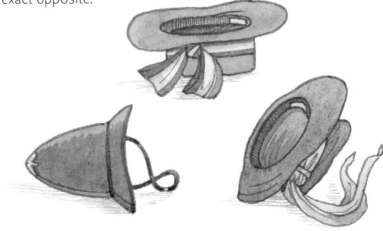

1910: Suffrajitsu

Fig. 1   Fig. 2   Fig. 3

SHE WAS ONLY FOUR FEET ELEVEN INCHES TALL, BUT EDITH GARRUD COULD THROW A POLICEMAN OVER HER SHOULDER, NO PROBLEM AT ALL. FOR EDITH HAD LEARNED THE ANCIENT MARTIAL ART OF JUJITSU.

Of course, the suffragettes didn't go around throwing policemen over their shoulders willy-nilly. But after being pushed around so violently and even beaten up by policemen on Black Friday, many suffragettes decided they ought to learn how to defend themselves.

Jujitsu (which, translated from Japanese, means "soft art") was perfect, being all about defense, not attack. The idea is to knock your attacker off balance, and then use their body weight to push or fling them to the ground. It is as much a science as a sport. By learning jujitsu, a woman, regardless of her size, could easily deflect an attack from a bigger, stronger man.

At the time, there was a craze for all things Japanese. Edith Garrud, along with her husband, William, had learned the skill of jujitsu from Mr. Edward William Barton-Wright, who had brought two Japanese jujitsu masters to Britain. Edith and William ran a martial arts school in London, where Edith gave self-defense lessons to women and children.

Soon suffragettes started attending, at first to learn how to fend off angry stage invaders and troublemakers at

Fig. 4   *Fig. 5*   *Fig. 6*

their speeches and rallies. But after the brutality of Black Friday, Edith began giving special classes exclusively to suffragettes.

Regularly writing for the *Suffragette* newspaper on the subject, with photographs and diagrams illustrating how to do the moves, Edith would describe the art of "twisting wrists, elbows, or knee joints the way they are not meant to go." Ouch!

A woman doing any sort of physical activity would have been a curiosity to many at this time, so a tiny policeman-throwing lady in a huge hat and long skirt caused a bit of a stir. Edith became quite famous, and cartoons were drawn of her fending off big, burly brutes

or hurling policemen over railings while others stood quivering nearby. Poems were written about her:

For women are learning ju-jitsu,
And throwing policemen about;
And when a man meets
With the women athletes
He'll have to be good — or get out.

Before long, journalists had coined the phrases "Ju-jit-suffragettes" and "Suffrajitsu."

It sounds amusing, but it shows the determination and preparedness of the suffragettes.

1911: The Suffragette in the Broom Closet

EMILY WILDING DAVISON WAS SMART. SHE WAS DETERMINED TO BREAK THE RULES MADE BY THE GOVERNMENT UNTIL THEY GAVE WOMEN THE VOTE. AND SHE WAS VERY GOOD AT BREAKING RULES.

The year 1911 was a "census" year in the U.K. A census is a way for the government to count how many people there are in the country and where they live. Absolutely everyone must be included, so every ten years since 1841, the head of every household has had to fill out a form and write the names of all the people who are living there or visiting on that particular census night.

This way, the government gets a good picture of the whole population and can make decisions on things like health care and education. It is against the law to refuse to fill out a census form or to mess it up by writing "VOTES FOR WOMEN" across it or "IF WOMEN DON'T COUNT, NEITHER SHALL THEY BE COUNTED." But that is exactly what some suffragettes did in 1911. This was very brave, as they faced a fine or even prison by doing it.

Some suffragettes found other ways to commit acts of civil disobedience. Throughout England, many decided to avoid being at home for the census and instead spent the night walking the streets. Some camped out on Wimbledon Common; others went to all-night concerts that were being specially held to encourage women to avoid the census. Many walked around and around Trafalgar Square, and some restaurants stayed open all night so the women could stop for a cup of tea to keep up their energy.

Some suffragettes declared their homes to be a "census-avoiding property" where no forms would be filled in. They invited women to stay the night, and some had twenty-five or more sleeping in their house. One resilient suffragette put on her winter coat and sat all night in her garden shed.

All this was to purposely mess up the government's system of getting information on the population.

Emily Wilding Davison had an even more brilliant idea: to hide in a broom closet in the Chapel of the Palace of Westminster (the building that houses Parliament).

And she did just that. Emily hid there until morning, with only some canned meat lozenges and lime juice to sustain her.

It sounds horrible, but by spending the night of April 2, 1911, in that closet, she could officially write on her census form that her place of residence was the Houses of Parliament. The 1911 census actually lists Emily Wilding Davidson (they spelled her name wrong) as "found hiding in crypt of Westminster Hall."

What a clever idea. Although women were not allowed to vote or to become MPs, through her actions, she knew her name would forever be linked to the Houses of Parliament.

Sadly, however, the name Emily Wilding Davison would be best remembered for a tragic event that took place two years later as the suffragettes continued to find new ways to protest.

1911: Acid, Ink, and Fire Bombs

BY 1911, THE SUPPORTERS OF WOMEN'S SUFFRAGE IN BRITAIN WERE THOROUGHLY FED UP. THEY FELT IGNORED BY THE GOVERNMENT — AND BY EVERYONE ELSE, FOR THAT MATTER. THEY NEEDED TO DO SOMETHING EXTREME.

Some members of the WSPU decided to take matters into their own hands, and across the country, attacks started to take place on, of all things, mailboxes.

Mailboxes made eye-catching targets. In the early 1900s, there were no computers, there was no Internet, and very few people owned a telephone; there was certainly no such thing as a cell phone. Writing letters was the only way to communicate, which made the Royal Mail a precious and vital part of everyday life; people depended on it. It is said that in those days you could receive a letter, write and post your response, and even receive a reply all on the same day. The suffragettes knew exactly what they were doing by destroying the mail. These mailbox attacks were designed to wake up the public and the government and force them to take women's suffrage seriously.

Some mailboxes were set on fire, and many more had ink or acid poured into them to destroy the letters

inside. The very first time a mailbox was set ablaze was in December 1911, when Emily Wilding Davison set not one, but three mailboxes on fire. Other suffragettes followed her example. Margaret Haig Mackworth (the second Viscountess Rhondda), known as the Welsh Boadicea, tried to blow up a mailbox with a homemade bomb. She was arrested, as was Rosa May Billinghurst for the same offense. Rosa never let her wheelchair get in the way of being an active militant suffragette and decorated her chair in the colors of the WSPU, with banners and ribbons proclaiming VOTES FOR WOMEN. She was arrested several times. Emily, Margaret, and Rosa were sent to prison, where they all went on hunger strike.

Many people were enraged by these women's acts, which they saw as a blatant disregard for the mail. They thought the militant suffragettes were a menace and favored a "Lock 'em up and throw away the key" approach.

At first, the leaders of the WSPU did not want to be seen as supporting such destruction, but it wasn't long before it was given the seal of approval by Emmeline Pankhurst herself. In 1912, she gave a big speech at the Royal Albert Hall in London in which she encouraged her supporters to "be militant in [their] own way" and do whatever they could to force the government to give votes to women. This was just the beginning of the assault on property.

1912: A Bigger Smash

IN 1912, WINDOW SMASHING BECAME OFFICIALLY APPROVED BY THE LEADERS OF THE WSPU.

Back in 1908, when Mary Leigh and Edith New had smashed the windows of 10 Downing Street, it had been very much an individual action. But by 1912, the breaking of windows had become organized, with coordinated attacks designed to cause as much damage and disruption as possible.

In 1911, MPs voted in favor of the Second Conciliation Bill, which would give more than one million women the vote. But before it could be made law, Prime Minister Asquith again interfered and changed it into a "Manhood Suffrage" bill, which instead focused on giving the vote to the millions of working-class men who still had no right to one. The women were angry to have been written out of the bill, and on November 21, 1911, they organized a massive window-breaking attack.

The sound of breaking glass could be heard coming from government buildings all over London, but this time some shops, hotels, newspaper offices, and gentlemen's clubs were attacked too. More than two hundred women and three men were arrested and sent to prison, and hundreds of pounds' worth of damage was reported.

Many suffragettes did not agree with window breaking, believing it was costing them support from the public, and left the WSPU to join other, nonmilitant suffrage groups. But Emmeline Pankhurst wasn't bothered in the slightest, declaring, "The smashing of windows is a time-honored method of showing displeasure in a political situation."

On March 1, 1912, at precisely 5:30 in the evening, elegantly dressed ladies whipped out miniature toffee hammers, a common kitchen item at the time, from their muffs and handbags and proceeded to calmly smash shopwindows in London. All along the fanciest streets in London came the piercing sound of metal hitting glass, followed by the angry shouts of shoppers and shopkeepers.

The WSPU was insistent that no one get injured in the attack, so the women were instructed how to break the glass so that it wouldn't rain splinters and shards down on themselves or on passersby.

Emmeline Pankhurst and her friend Ethel Smyth both took part and were among the 126 women arrested. The cost of all that broken glass came to more than 5,000 pounds (worth about 500,000 pounds today), and for days afterward some of the fanciest shops in London had boarded-up windows. Some smaller shops even put up signs in their windows begging the suffragettes not to smash them. Once again, the public was getting fed up. But women like Emmeline and Ethel were not about to relent.

1912: "Shout, Shout, Up with Your Song!"

E THEL SMYTH LOVED GOLF AND COULD OFTEN BE SEEN ON THE GOLF COURSE DRESSED HEAD TO TOE IN TWEED WITH HER HAT ON CROOKED. IT WAS MUSIC, HOWEVER, THAT WAS HER LIFE.

Ethel lived for music: the rhythm of it, the power of it, the conversations between notes. Her father had been opposed to her becoming a composer, but that didn't stop his daughter. It just made her more determined. She studied hard and wrote all sorts of music, including many operas, and became famous around the world.

Then, in 1910, she met and fell in love with Emmeline Pankhurst. Ethel was so captivated by Emmeline's zeal for victory in winning the vote for women that she declared she would give up her musical career for two whole years and instead dedicate that time to the WSPU. She joined immediately and soon put her talents to good use by writing the song that would become the WSPU's anthem; not just a song, but "a hymn and a call to battle": "The March of the Women."

There is something very special about singing in a group. Raising voices in song creates a magical feeling and a sense of belonging. I guess this is why people

sing at soccer matches or in church. You don't even need to be a good singer, as you can mingle your voice with others and still make a joyful noise.

The suffragettes loved to sing together. It made them feel connected in their struggle to win the vote. And there was no better song than "The March of the Women" to make them feel good about themselves. The lyrics, written by Cicely Hamilton, speak of fearlessness and strength, bravery and glory: inspiring words to keep spirits high.

In 1912, encouraged by Emmeline, Ethel threw a stone through the window of a leading politician opposed to women's suffrage. She was promptly arrested and sentenced to two months in Holloway Prison. A visiting friend remembered watching the other suffragette prisoners parading around the prison yard singing their "war chant," "The March of the Women," with gusto, while above them from her cell window, Ethel enthusiastically conducted with a toothbrush.

The following year, when Ethel started to go deaf, she stopped composing music. Instead she wrote books, but her contribution to music was remembered when, in 1922, she became the first female composer to receive the British title of dame.

The March of the Women.

Dedicated to the Women's Social and Political Union

PRICE ONE PENNY ETHEL SMYTH. Mus. Doc.

(Band)

1. Shout, shout, up with your song! Cry with the wind, for the dawn is break-ing.

March, march, swing you a-long, Wide blows our ban-ner and hope is wak-ing. Song with its sto-ry, dreams with their glo-ry,

Lo! They call and glad is their word. For-ward!

Hark how it swells, Thun-der of free-dom, the voice of the Lord!

2.

Long, long, we in the past,
Cowered in dread from the light of Heaven.
Strong, strong stand we at last,
Fearless in faith and with sight new given.
Strength with its beauty, life with its duty,
(Hear the voice, oh, hear and obey).
These, these beckon us on,
Open your eyes to the blaze of day!

3.

Comrades, ye who have dared.
First in the battle to strive and sorrow.
Scorned, spurned, naught have ye cared,
Raising your eyes to a wider morrow.
Ways that are weary, days that are dreary,
Toil and pain by faith ye have borne.
Hail, hail, victors ye stand,
Wearing the wreath that the brave have worn!

4.

Life, strife, these two are one!
Naught can ye win but by faith and daring.
On, on, that ye have done,
But for the work of today preparing.
Firm in reliance, laugh a defiance,
(Laugh in hope, for sure is the end).
March, march, many as one,
Shoulder to shoulder and friend to friend!

1913: A Game of Cat and Mouse

FORCE-FEEDING NOT ONLY WAS HUGELY UNPOPULAR WITH THE PUBLIC AND POLITICIANS, BUT IT ALSO WAS NOT REALLY WORKING.

The suffragette prisoners were ever more determined to stand united in their struggle, and more and more women and men were joining in the hunger strike as soon as they were imprisoned.

Terrified of the backlash from the public should a suffragette die in prison, the government came up with its sneakiest tactic yet. In April 1913, a new law was hurriedly passed. It was called the Temporary Discharge for Ill Health Act.

But here is why it was so sneaky. Prisoners would be allowed to go on hunger strike, refusing food and even water, until they became weak and ill. Then they would be released from jail and allowed to go home or stay in a safe house for, say, two weeks or longer.

At home they would begin eating normally once more and in time regain their health and strength, at which point they would be expected to return to prison and complete their sentence. Of course, no one ever went back to prison voluntarily. Once out, the suffragettes did their very best to stay out; some went into hiding, while others even left the country.

The police had to keep watch over released prisoners, spying on their every move, ready to pounce and rearrest them when their health had improved.

What a dreadfully dreary process. A prison sentence of a couple of months could be stretched out over a year or more, with the prisoner constantly yo-yoing back and forth to jail, threatening his or her physical and mental well-being.

This law became known as the Cat and Mouse Act. The government was like a cat playing with its prey, a suffragette, the mouse: trapping it, letting it go, then pouncing on it again and again until the poor mouse was too weak to fight back.

The WSPU released a poster showing an illustration of a mean-looking cat with blood-stained fangs. In its jaws hung the limp, listless body of a suffragette (the mouse), draped in the purple, green, and white colors of the union. It was a powerful and sinister image.

The first prisoner to be released under the act was not officially a suffragette but a man named Hugh Franklin.

Prisoners (Temporary Discharge for Ill-health) Act, 1913

AN ACT

TO

Provide for the Temporary Discharge of Prisoners whose further detention in prison is undesirable on account of the condition of their Health.

25th April 1913

Hugh was from a very rich family. He was studying engineering at Cambridge University, but he gave up his studies after hearing Mrs. Pankhurst, Mrs. Pethick-Lawrence, and Christabel Pankhurst speaking at his college in 1909.

Hugh was already a firm believer in women's equality, but after this encounter with "the Militants," he decided to dedicate all his time to joining them in acts of civil disobedience.

Being a man, he wasn't allowed to join the WSPU, so he joined the Men's Political Union for Women's Enfranchisement and the Men's League for Woman's Suffrage. He also helped form the Jewish League for Woman Suffrage.

He was one of the four men arrested on Black Friday, although on that occasion he wasn't sent to jail. Hugh blamed Winston Churchill for the violence and abuse the suffragettes received that day, and he later attacked Churchill with a whip. For that, he did go to prison.

In total, Hugh went to jail three times in support of winning votes for women. The second time was for throwing a stone at Churchill's house, and the third was for setting fire to a railway carriage at London's Harrow train station.

For that, he got nine months in jail and went on hunger strike. Hugh was force-fed more than a hundred times before the government released him under the Cat and Mouse Act.

The second person to be released just so happened to be Hugh's girlfriend, Elsie Duval. Elsie was from a family of avid suffragists and had been in jail for loitering. On hunger strike, she was force-fed nine times before being released in very poor health. Elsie and Hugh ran off to Belgium to avoid being rearrested, and they didn't return to Britain for more than a year.

Cruel as it was, however, even the Cat and Mouse Act did nothing to pause the fight for votes for women.

1913: Capturing the Monument

UNDAUNTED BY THE GOVERNMENT'S RUTH-LESS TACTICS, THE SUFFRAGETTES FOUND INCREASINGLY INVENTIVE WAYS OF BRINGING ATTENTION TO THEIR FIGHT.

By acting in secret, they continued to outwit the police who were constantly taken by surprise, even when major events or landmarks were targeted.

On the morning of Friday, April 18, 1913, Ethel Spark and Gertrude Shaw each bought a ticket to go up the Monument in London, the tower built to commemorate the Great Fire of London.

Together they climbed the 311 steps to the top, where they politely chatted with the two attendants on duty that day.

While the men were distracted, the women managed to trap them in their office and shut the door to the viewing platform, locking it tight with two iron poles that they had smuggled in under their clothes.

Then, quick as a flash, they hauled down the City of London flag that was flying high on the flagpole and replaced it with the purple, green, and white flag of the WSPU.

Next, a large banner that read DEATH OR VICTORY in huge letters was unfurled over the railings, along with streamers of purple, green, and white that billowed in the breeze.

When a large enough crowd had gathered to see what all the fuss was about, Ethel and Gertrude let loose hundreds of VOTES FOR WOMEN leaflets that fluttered down to the streets below.

Eventually, the police arrived, but they needed an enormous sledgehammer to break down the door. It took some time, but eventually they reached the women and arrested them.

Ethel and Gertrude were taken to Bow Street Magistrates' Court but were released without charge. Perhaps the magistrate felt it was not worth the trouble of putting these two annoying women in prison, especially if they were then to go on hunger strike.

It was another successful publicity stunt by the WSPU, whose members were delighted with themselves for causing such disruption. The *Votes for Women* newspaper gleefully reported the incident as another success "to add to the list of triumphs of female ingenuity."

But the members of the NUWSS were impatient with the WSPU. All the violence and destruction caused by a few militant suffragettes was making the public and the government angry and was not, they felt, helping the cause.

Most of the women and men trying to win the vote were law-abiding suffragists, not lawbreaking suffragettes, but the lawbreakers were getting all the attention.

Something big needed to be done to show the country that not everyone was smashing windows, blowing up mailboxes, or locking up attendants in the name of women's suffrage.

In fact, some suffragists believed that words would, in the end, prove more effective than deeds when it came to winning the vote.

1913: The Pilgrims Make Progress

ON THE SAME DAY THAT THE WSPU WAS STORMING THE MONUMENT, THE NUWSS WAS PLANNING A PEACEFUL PUBLICITY CAMPAIGN.

The Scottish suffragists had had their own march from Edinburgh to London in 1912, and in the summer of 1913, it was decided that an even bigger pilgrimage of women would march from all corners of England and Wales, from Land's End to Newcastle, to meet at Hyde Park in London.

Starting from the farthest districts on June 18 and 19, groups of women and a small number of men set off from seventeen towns and cities.

It would take weeks to walk that far, and the NUWSS encouraged as many of its 100,000 members as possible to take part. They were not expected to walk the whole route, just join in for chunks of it, to show a steady, strong troop. Some rode bicycles and others rode horses, but the pilgrimage was not supposed to be a big, showy carnival parade. Quite the opposite: this was about talking to people along the way.

Even so, they wanted to be recognized by the public, so they wore a sort of uniform: white, gray, black, or navy skirts, with matching blouses, and hats decorated in the red, green, and white of the NUWSS. It was a simple uniform so that any member of the union could join in without having to buy a new outfit.

The pilgrimage was a brilliant idea. The suffragists were able to chat with people face-to-face, discussing their thoughts and ideas about women's suffrage as they passed through the towns and villages on their journey.

It was mostly friendly; sometimes the whole town would turn out to see the suffragists and cheer them on. Children would present them with flowers, and the atmosphere was inquisitive and jolly.

Not everyone was so welcoming, though. As they passed through some towns, the women were pelted with stones, eggs, mud, and even great big cabbages. They had their hats ripped off, were pushed off their bikes, and had their luggage thrown in rivers. In some towns, groups of working-class men protected the women from being mobbed by hooligans, including university students who considered these women a joke. Not having the vote themselves yet, these working men were more sympathetic to the cause.

When they reached Hyde Park on July 26, they were dusty, sunburned, and tired but in a triumphant mood. The pilgrimage had been a huge success. They had collected more than 8,000 pounds (worth about 900,000 pounds today) for the union, given out half a million leaflets, and enrolled thousands of new members.

The NUWSS seemed to be back on track for victory, and without recourse to the violence or lawbreaking of the WSPU, which continued.

1913: Burning Down the House

ON MARCH 3, 1912, A BRITISH MIDWIFE NAMED ELLEN PITFIELD SET FIRE TO A BASKET OF WOOD IN A POST OFFICE.

She then threw a brick through its window—and so began the next and most devastatingly destructive phase of the WSPU's campaign of protest against the government's unwillingness to bring about political change.

Emmeline Pankhurst had called upon the suffragettes to destroy the one thing that in her opinion men valued most: property. She also made very clear that no human life should be harmed in such attacks, writing, "I have never advised the destruction of life, but of property, YES!"

At first the homes of leading anti-suffragists were targeted, but before long, all sorts of public and private property went up in flames at the strike of a match lit by a suffragette. Often, while investigating the smoldering ruins, police would find little notes reading "Votes for women" or "Stop torturing our comrades in prison," which left little doubt as to who the attackers had been.

A theater in Dublin where Prime Minister Asquith was due to give a speech was attacked by Mary Leigh and Gladys Evans, and although only the curtain went up in smoke, each woman received a prison sentence of five years.

By 1913, rail carriages had been set ablaze; the orchid house at Kew Gardens burned to the ground; an Oxford boathouse, a cricket pavilion, and a racecourse grandstand all destroyed or damaged by fire. On December 26, 1913, the *Suffragette* listed over one hundred of the more serious attacks on property that had taken place that year and had been attributed to the suffragettes.

Suffragettes had even attempted to blow up a country house that was being built for David Lloyd George, who as chancellor of the exchequer was an important member of the government.

Emmeline Pankhurst claimed full responsibility for inciting the bombers. This time she was sentenced to three years in jail.

The suffragettes were attracting more and more attention, including from the authorities. The headquarters of the WSPU was raided by police, and "troublemaker" suffragettes were put under surveillance.

Some suffragettes, including Christabel Pankhurst, had escaped to Paris when they were released from jail under the Cat and Mouse Act. They could not be allowed to beat the system in this way, so by the end of the year, force-feeding was reintroduced for hunger-striking prisoners. Meanwhile, any sympathy the public had had for the suffragettes was fast running out.

1913: A Death at the Races

EMILY WILDING DAVISON WAS FIERCE AND FEARLESS. AS A MEMBER OF THE WSPU, SHE DEDICATED YEARS OF HER LIFE TO THE CAMPAIGN TO WIN VOTES FOR WOMEN.

She was a bit of a loose cannon. A dedicated risk-taker, Emily would, it seemed, do anything in the fight for women's suffrage. This irked the leaders of the WSPU, who had on occasion tried to distance themselves from her more extreme actions.

In 1909, she quit her job as a teacher to become a full-time warrior suffragette. She threw stones, smashed windows, set fire to things. She once attacked a church minister, mistaking him for David Lloyd George, then chancellor of the exchequer and a senior member of the government. Some people think she even planted a bomb in his empty house.

The Epsom Derby was one of the most splendid and important races of the year for any horse-racing fan. On June 4, 1913, thousands of spectators were gathered to watch, among them Emily Wilding Davison.

Before the race began, Emily found herself a spot with a great view at the front of the crowd on the bend known as Tattenham Corner. She had two suffragette flags hidden in her clothing and, folded neatly in her left hand, a silk scarf in the purple, green, and white colors of the WSPU, imprinted with the motto VOTES FOR WOMEN.

As the horses thundered toward her, she calmly ducked under the barrier and quite deliberately walked right out onto the racetrack. Emily stood facing the horses as they sped past, her eyes fixed on one horse in particular: Anmer, the king's horse.

Emily Davison went to prison nine times, where she joined the hunger strike and was brutally force-fed. Once, she barricaded herself into her cell to avoid force-feeding, and was hosed down with freezing-cold water until she felt like she was drowning. Another time, she threw herself down the iron stairs in the prison to deliberately hurt herself and bring attention to the plight of her fellow hunger strikers. But no one, not even her closest friends, could imagine what she would do next.

She raised her arms as Anmer hurtled toward her. King George V, Queen Mary, and hundreds of spectators watched in horror as the horse suddenly collided with Emily, who was tossed head over heels, tumbling through the air. Such was the force of the impact that Anmer also somersaulted, catapulting his jockey, Herbert Jones, from his back. The horse crashed to the ground, then stumbled back to his feet unharmed.

Emily and Herbert lay motionless on the track as the race continued. People rushed to help, and the two were taken to the hospital.

Herbert, who wasn't badly injured, made a full recovery, but Emily never regained consciousness: her skull had been fractured, and she died of her injuries four days later.

At the time, most people thought Emily had purposely tried to kill herself by trying to grab hold of the king's horse in a crazy publicity stunt. But many historians think differently now and don't believe she had intended to die. Of course we will never know for sure, but the folded silk scarf in her hand could be a clue to her real intentions. One thought is that she was attempting to throw the scarf over the neck of the horse as it charged past her: the sight of the king's horse crossing the finish line draped in a suffragette scarf emblazoned with the words VOTES FOR WOMEN would have been the greatest feat the suffragettes had ever achieved. Perhaps Emily simply misjudged the speed of the galloping horse or her own position on the track.

Whatever the truth, there is no doubt Emily wanted to draw maximum attention to the campaign for women's votes. The race was being filmed, and she managed to place herself in the perfect spot to be captured on camera. By the end of the day, blurry black-and-white images of her actions were flickering across cinema screens all over the country.

Her funeral procession through London was a tremendous spectacle watched by thousands, both those crowding the streets as it passed and those in cinemas watching the newsreel footage.

Emily Wilding Davison had become the most famous suffragette in the world.

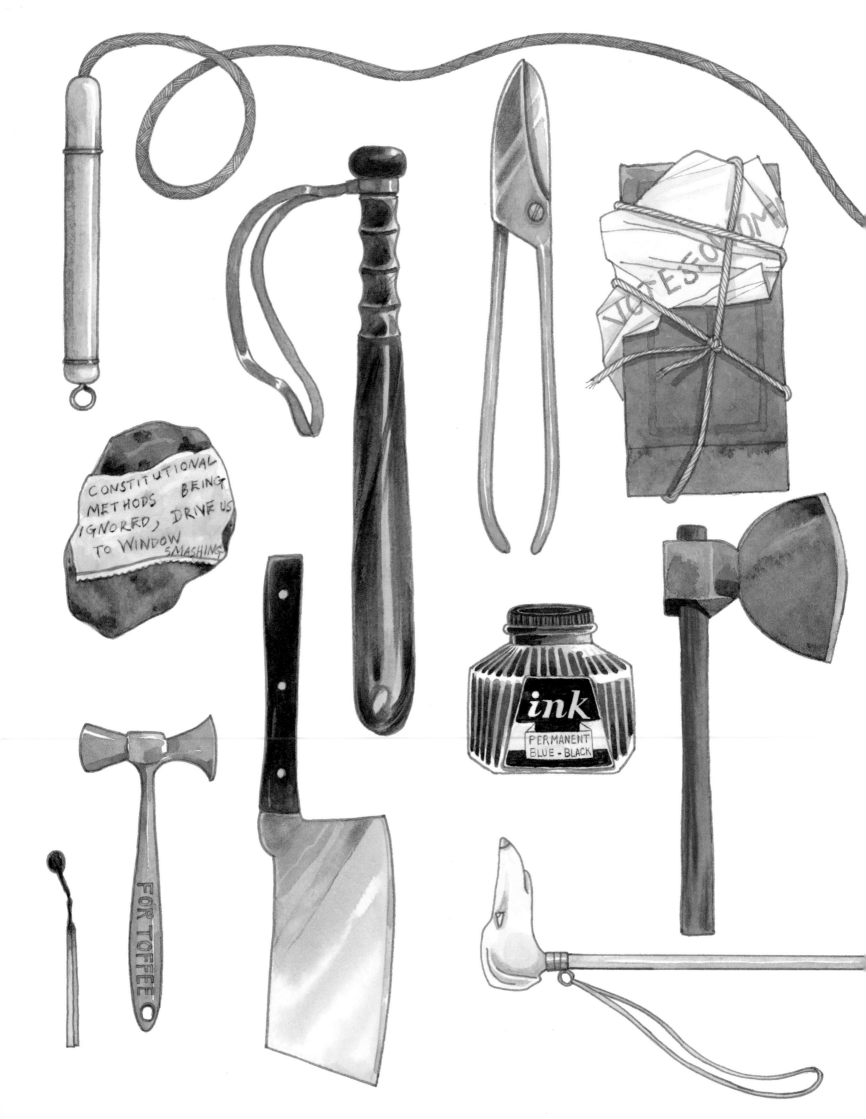

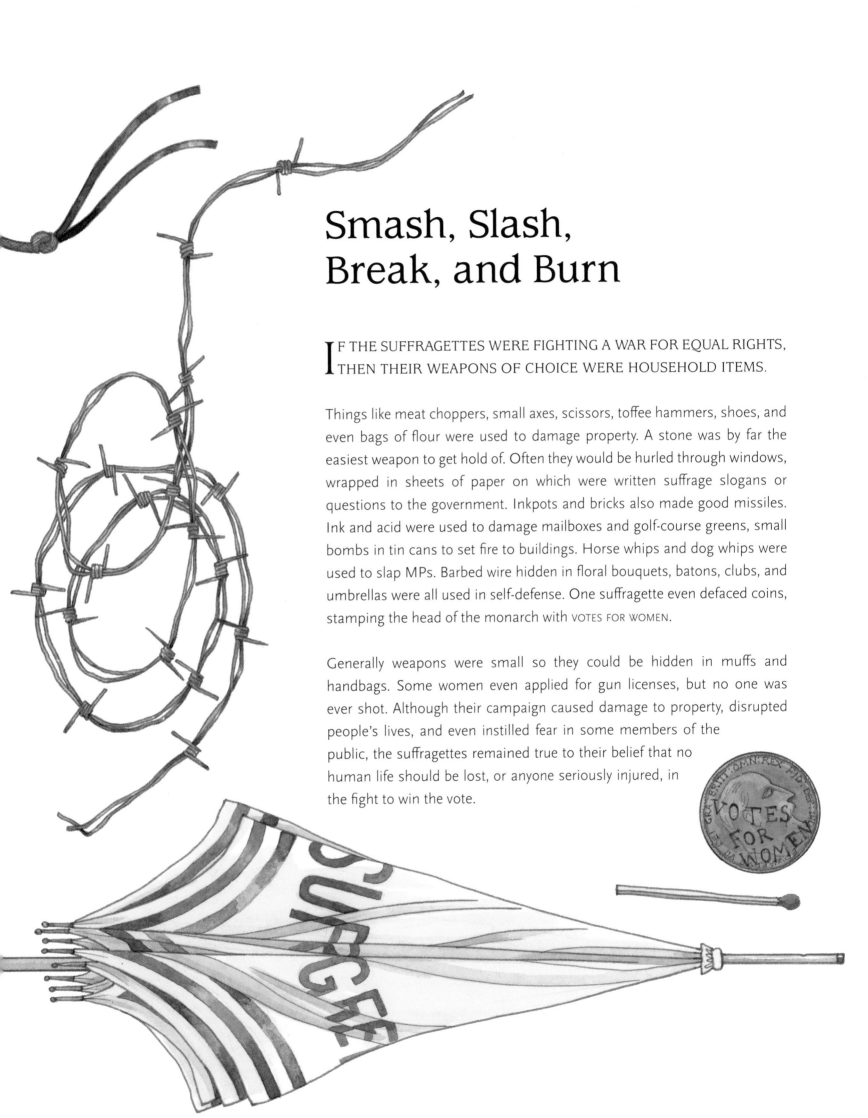

Smash, Slash, Break, and Burn

I F THE SUFFRAGETTES WERE FIGHTING A WAR FOR EQUAL RIGHTS, THEN THEIR WEAPONS OF CHOICE WERE HOUSEHOLD ITEMS.

Things like meat choppers, small axes, scissors, toffee hammers, shoes, and even bags of flour were used to damage property. A stone was by far the easiest weapon to get hold of. Often they would be hurled through windows, wrapped in sheets of paper on which were written suffrage slogans or questions to the government. Inkpots and bricks also made good missiles. Ink and acid were used to damage mailboxes and golf-course greens, small bombs in tin cans to set fire to buildings. Horse whips and dog whips were used to slap MPs. Barbed wire hidden in floral bouquets, batons, clubs, and umbrellas were all used in self-defense. One suffragette even defaced coins, stamping the head of the monarch with VOTES FOR WOMEN.

Generally weapons were small so they could be hidden in muffs and handbags. Some women even applied for gun licenses, but no one was ever shot. Although their campaign caused damage to property, disrupted people's lives, and even instilled fear in some members of the public, the suffragettes remained true to their belief that no human life should be lost, or anyone seriously injured, in the fight to win the vote.

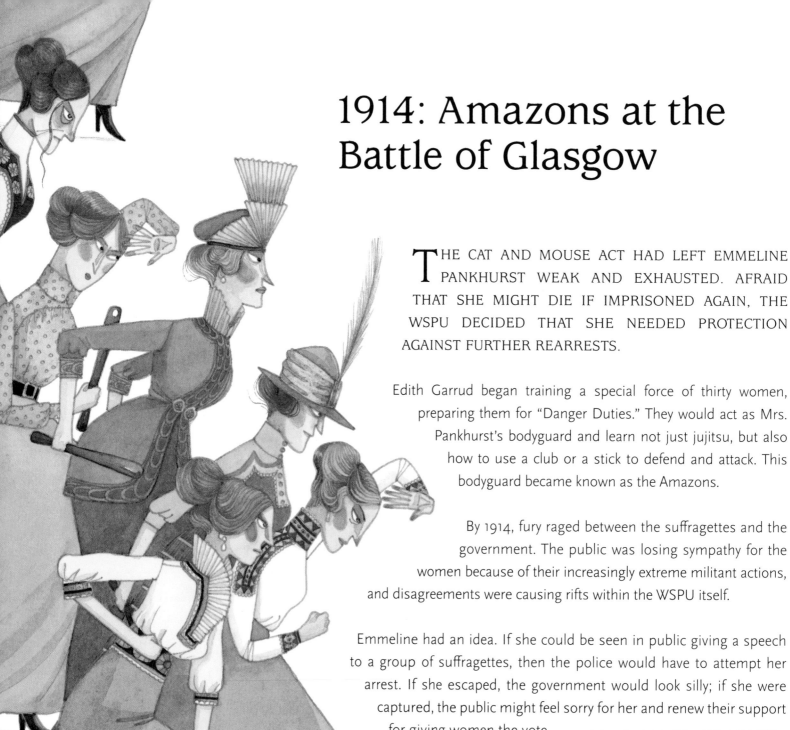

1914: Amazons at the Battle of Glasgow

THE CAT AND MOUSE ACT HAD LEFT EMMELINE PANKHURST WEAK AND EXHAUSTED. AFRAID THAT SHE MIGHT DIE IF IMPRISONED AGAIN, THE WSPU DECIDED THAT SHE NEEDED PROTECTION AGAINST FURTHER REARRESTS.

Edith Garrud began training a special force of thirty women, preparing them for "Danger Duties." They would act as Mrs. Pankhurst's bodyguard and learn not just jujitsu, but also how to use a club or a stick to defend and attack. This bodyguard became known as the Amazons.

By 1914, fury raged between the suffragettes and the government. The public was losing sympathy for the women because of their increasingly extreme militant actions, and disagreements were causing rifts within the WSPU itself.

Emmeline had an idea. If she could be seen in public giving a speech to a group of suffragettes, then the police would have to attempt her arrest. If she escaped, the government would look silly; if she were captured, the public might feel sorry for her and renew their support for giving women the vote.

A suffragette meeting was to be held in March 1914 at St. Andrew's Hall in Glasgow, Scotland. Rumors abounded that Emmeline, who was in hiding after her most recent release from prison under the Cat and Mouse Act, would be there to make a speech.

The venue was jam-packed. The police were taking no chances of letting Mrs. Pankhurst slip through their fingers and had surrounded the building. Fifty more policemen were hiding in the basement below. It seemed impossible that Emmeline could slink past them unnoticed.

But just when all hope of hearing Mrs. Pankhurst speak that day was fading, Emmeline miraculously appeared onstage. It was not a miracle or even a clever magic trick; she had simply worn a disguise, bought a ticket like everyone else, and swished into the hall right under the noses of the waiting police. To the delight of the audience, she began her speech:

"Equal justice for men and women, equal political justice, equal legal justice, equal industrial justice, and equal social justice!"

But her speech was cut short by the ominous sound of the police rushing up from the basement. One of the Amazons whipped out a pistol, and shots rang out. Fortunately, they were blanks. Startled but uninjured, the police stumbled onto the stage. Twenty-five Amazons, armed with the sticks and clubs they had hidden in their dresses, formed a circle around Mrs. Pankhurst.

The first policeman to clamber onto the platform was ensnared and tangled in the barbed wire hidden by the suffragettes among the pretty floral garlands decorating the stage. Several plainclothes policemen who were hiding in the audience now made a move to grab Mrs. Pankhurst but were beaten back by ladies with umbrellas. The crowd booed and jeered as the police walloped the Amazons with their truncheons. Chairs and tables were flung about as the battle raged on.

The Amazons put up a brave fight, but they were soon overpowered by the police, and Emmeline was captured and dragged from the hall, tattered and bruised from the struggle. The government was victorious; Mrs. Pankhurst was back in prison.

But the public was appalled. Emmeline had been right. After what became known as the Battle of Glasgow, people once again renewed their sympathy and support for the fight to win women the vote.

1914: Don't Forget the Workers

FASHIONABLE LADIES THROWING STONES IS THE POPULAR IMAGE OF WHO THE SUFFRAGETTES WERE, BUT THAT IS JUST ONE SIDE OF THE SUFFRAGE CAMPAIGN.

Thousands of suffragettes and suffragists were working-class people, some from extremely poor backgrounds. These women didn't have much money or free time, but they gave a great deal of support to the fight for their rights.

Some of the suffrage organizations were concerned only with winning the right for women to vote on equal terms with men. Not all men had the vote, however, so in 1914, that meant only upper- and middle-class women who were well educated or owned their own home would be given the right to vote.

Working-class women were rightly disgruntled. They wanted votes for *all* women and men, regardless of class, education, or wealth. They risked a lot by being involved with the suffragists, and particularly with the suffragettes.

Many of the poorest working women would get only one day off work a week, but they would give up that day to join protest marches and processions. A working-class woman involved in a skirmish with the police could lose her job and face destitution as a result. Poor women who were arrested would never be able to pay a fine and so would inevitably end up being sent to prison. Sometimes these women might be the only person in their household bringing home a wage; thus prison could mean their children went without proper food and care for months, not to mention the shame and rejection the women faced from their communities or families, many of whom disapproved of their actions.

Still, many working-class women knew that the change needed to allow them to take control of their own lives would come about only when women played a part in politics and had an equal voice in governing the country. At the beginning of the 1900s, nearly 30,000 women from the northwest textile factories and mills had signed a petition demanding better pay and working conditions. This is what had prompted Emmeline Pankhurst to create the WSPU in the first place.

But by 1914, the increasingly violent and militant actions of certain members of the WSPU were causing squabbles and disapproval among the different suffrage organizations. The WSPU, which had started as a union to support working women's rights, had broadened to attract women of all social classes, rich and poor, since all women were excluded from the exercise of the parliamentary vote. Emmeline and Christabel also insisted that the WSPU be independent and not allied to any of the men's political parties of the day, including the Labor Party, even though this party was more sympathetic to the cause of votes for women.

Sylvia Pankhurst—Emmeline's younger daughter—did not agree with this approach, instead wanting to ally the WSPU more closely with the socialist movement. She formed her own group, the East London Federation of the Suffragettes (ELFS). The ELFS, contrary to WSPU policy, included both women and men members and supported Labor Party candidates who were running for election to parliament.

In January 1914, Sylvia was expelled from the WSPU due to her disagreements with Emmeline and Christabel. Along with Minnie Lansbury, Melvina Walker, and Julia Scurr, Sylvia refocused on the social issues affecting poor women.

VOTES FOR WORKERS

1914: "Slasher" Mary and the Art Attacks

MARY RICHARDSON LOVED ART, WHICH AT FIRST GLANCE MAKES WHAT SHE DID SEEM VERY STRANGE.

On March 10, 1914, Mary went to the National Gallery in London. There was one particular painting she wanted to see: *Venus at Her Mirror* by Diego Velázquez, painted in 1647. The gallery had bought it for the then-enormous sum of 45,000 pounds.

One year earlier, two suffragettes had attacked fourteen paintings at Manchester Art Gallery, smashing their glass and frames.

The National Gallery was taking no chances with its purchase: two security guards were positioned next to the painting, which was displayed behind a thick panel of glass for extra protection.

Mary stood in front of the painting, pretending to draw it in a sketchbook. Hidden up her sleeve was a meat chopper. But the two guards were not budging, and she began to think she would have no chance of getting close enough to attack the picture.

Then, to her surprise, one of the guards got up and wandered off for his lunch. At the same time, the other guard got out a newspaper and began to read it. With his face hidden by the paper, he didn't notice as Mary stepped forward and took a violent swing at the *Venus*. The meat chopper shattered the protective glass.

Mary thought she would instantly be grabbed by the newspaper-reading guard, but instead he was looking up at the skylight, wrongly thinking the window had been smashed.

Mary seized her chance and got in "five lovely shots" with the chopper, slashing the canvas across the back and shoulders of Venus's body.

Another guard now realized what was happening and ran to stop her, but he slipped and fell on the polished floor. Mary couldn't believe her luck. She got in a few more slashes before she was eventually grabbed and arrested. But the painting had been severely damaged.

People were utterly disgusted and appalled, horrified that someone would want to destroy art.

Mary was indignant, and responded, "I have tried to destroy the picture of the most beautiful woman in mythological history as a protest against the government for destroying Mrs. Pankhurst, who is the most beautiful character in modern history. . . . You can get another picture, but you cannot get another life. . . . They are killing Mrs. Pankhurst."

Later that year, things reached the boiling point. Just being seen in purple, green, and white could get a suffragette attacked by a raging member of the public. And if you were a man who supported votes for women, you could find yourself being dunked in a pond or lake, which is exactly what happened to the Reverend C. A. Wills after he had heckled Lloyd George.

But by August 1914, an even greater threat was looming.

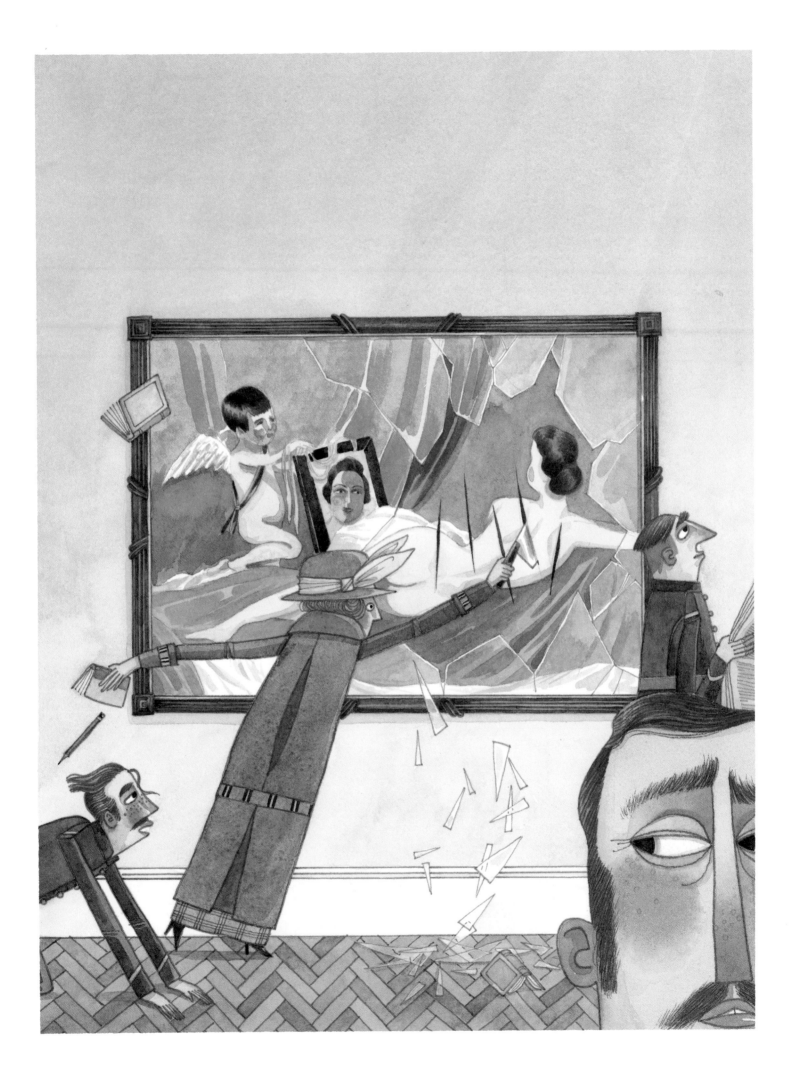

ON AUGUST 4, 1914, THE DARKNESS OF WORLD WAR I DESCENDED AS BRITAIN BEGAN ITS BLOODY CONFLICT WITH GERMANY.

Almost overnight, the whole campaign for women's suffrage changed, and the violent militant actions of the suffragettes came to an abrupt end.

By August 6, Millicent Fawcett and the leaders of the

Millicent urged its members to "prove themselves worthy of citizenship, whether our claim (as women) to it be recognized or not."

By August 10, the government agreed to an amnesty with the WSPU, releasing all suffrage prisoners, in jail or out (under the Cat and Mouse Act), from their sentences. Suddenly the campaign to win the vote took second place to the more urgent campaign to win

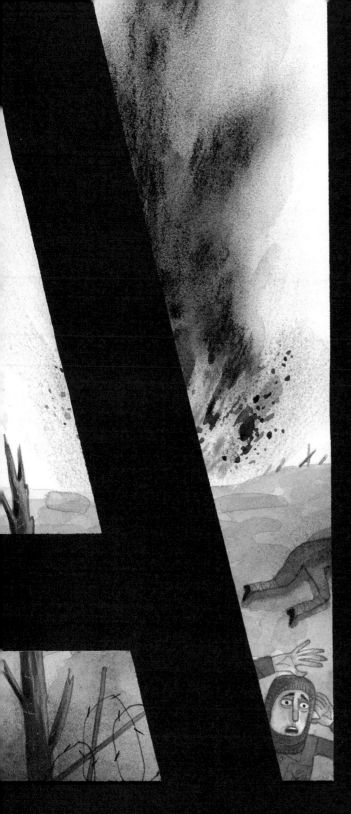

Emmeline Pankhurst wholeheartedly supported the war and urged the members of the WSPU to do the same, declaring, "What is the use of fighting for a vote if we have not got a country to vote in?"

By the middle of September 1914, more than a quarter of a million men had joined up to fight in France and Belgium. The newspaper *Votes for Women* announced, "Work of all kinds will want doing, and women will have

When the U.S. joined the war in 1917, American suffragists were divided. Some chose to follow the British example, hoping to gain support through their patriotism. Others used the war as part of their campaign, picketing the White House and highlighting the contradiction of fighting for a democracy that denied them the vote.

1915: For Men Must Fight and Women Must Work

AS THE WAR THUNDERED ON, MORE AND MORE MEN JOINED THE FIGHT. CONSEQUENTLY, THE WORKFORCE — ESSENTIAL TO KEEPING THE COUNTRY RUNNING — DWINDLED. THERE WAS AN URGENT NEED FOR WORKERS TO FILL THE JOBS VACATED BY MEN.

There was no shortage of women willing to work, but employers were reluctant to give women the jobs previously occupied by men. They thought the war might be over soon and the men safely home. Besides, they believed women were probably not capable of taking on men's work.

This conundrum brought about a rather strange alliance between two former enemies.

The government was all too aware of the influence Emmeline Pankhurst had had in recruiting women to win the vote. Might she be useful in the fight to win the war? The king himself asked the government if Mrs. Pankhurst could be effective in showing the public that a workforce of women was a good idea.

Emmeline was given a grant of 2,000 pounds by the government—a huge sum of money in 1915—to organize a great parade of women. This time they would be marching not for the right to vote but for the right to work and serve the country in its hour of great need.

Mrs. Pankhurst was more than enthusiastic, and with the support of the WSPU, the "Women's War Work" demonstration was organized within two weeks.

On July 17, 1915, she led a procession of more than 30,000 women and ninety marching bands through the streets of London in lashing rain and whipping wind. The women walked proudly, watched by more than 100,000 spectators.

Unlike the previous marches and demonstrations organized by the WSPU, this time there were no green, white, and purple flags or banners. Instead the marchers waved the red, white, and blue of the Union Jack.

Tables had been set up along the route as recruitment stations where women could register their interest in working to help win the war. It was a great success, and women from all classes and backgrounds eagerly signed up.

In a speech to the assembled crowds, David Lloyd George, the government minister of munitions, spoke of the urgency of employing women in full-time work, particularly in the munitions factories. An army needs ammunition to be victorious. The women were pleased to help.

1915–1918: Canaries and Penguins Help Win the War

MAKING BOMBS IS DIFFICULT, HIGHLY SKILLED WORK, AS WELL AS EXTREMELY DANGEROUS. BUT WOMEN WERE PREPARED TO TAKE THE RISKS.

Factories and employers had realized the need to employ women, and by the end of the war, it is estimated that more than a million women were working in munitions factories in the U.K. and the U.S. They played a crucial role in keeping the army supplied with bombs and bullets.

Along with the risk of accidental explosions, another serious hazard was poisoning by the chemicals used to make the explosives—including TNT, which turned workers' skin bright yellow and their hair green, and so earned them the nickname the Canaries. Although these alarming symptoms wore off in time, other effects of working with such dangerous chemicals resulted in the death of some women.

Certain safety precautions were introduced, including face masks, protective clothing, and wooden shoes. A blow from anything metal could detonate the TNT, so there was a ban on all metal items on the factory floor, such as hairpins or jewelry. And there were no matches allowed; a worker could be sent to jail for bringing a match to work. But accidents still happened.

Of course, working-class women had always worked, but now with so many men away fighting in the war, they had much wider opportunities available to them. This brought with it the chance to earn more money.

For the first time, women became police officers and firefighters, railway porters and ticket collectors, carpenters and electricians, streetcar and bus conductors, even chimney sweeps and gravediggers—all jobs that had previously been thought of exclusively as "men's work."

The fancy London department store Harrods employed several women as truck drivers, commenting that they were "good, careful drivers, who had few accidents and were much less tired at the end of the working day than the male drivers had been."

But the women didn't just drive the vehicles; they learned how to fix them, too: women became welders, mechanics, and engineers.

Women also worked in agriculture: the Women's Land Army was formed in 1917 in the U.K. to provide the country with enough food to survive the war.

Nurses played a vital part in caring for soldiers both at home and overseas on the battlefields, where the fighting raged on. There were 45,000 British and American nurses serving in World War I.

The war also saw the first women join the armed forces—not to fight alongside the men, but to provide practical support. In Britain, the WVR (Women's Volunteer Reserve) was founded in 1914, right at the start of the war. The WAAC (Women's Auxiliary Army Corps), the WRNS (Women's Royal Naval Service), and the WRAF (Women's Royal Air Force) were all founded between 1917 and 1918. In the United States, women were allowed to enlist in the navy beginning in 1917 and were known colloquially as yeomanettes. They were not allowed in the army, though many were part of the Army Nursing Corps.

The WRAF trained women to be air mechanics, but they were not allowed to actually fly the planes into war, which earned them the nickname the Penguins because they were "flightless." It would have been quite unthinkable in previous generations to see women in so many "male" jobs, let alone in the armed forces, but the war offered these opportunities—and women were ready to take them.

Seeing women in these roles made the U.K. and U.S. governments' position against giving them the vote increasingly ridiculous. As the headline of the suffragette newspaper *Votes for Women* put it in December 1915, "Why Not Votes for Two as Well as Jobs for Two?" If a woman was as capable as a man of doing a job, surely she was as capable of voting.

1918: The Vote Won

VICTORY AT LAST! AFTER CAMPAIGNING FOR MORE THAN SIXTY YEARS, WOMEN IN THE U.K. HAD FINALLY WON THE VOTE.

On February 6, 1918, the Representation of the People Act became law in the U.K. All men over the age of twenty-one, the age at that time when someone was considered an adult, received the right to vote. Men in the military could vote at nineteen. This was the first time in British history that all men, regardless of wealth or status, were given political equality with one another.

But victory for women came with restrictions. To qualify to vote, a woman had to be over the age of thirty. In addition, she had to own her own home or be married to a property owner. She also had the right to vote if she was a university graduate or if she was paying an annual rent of five pounds or more on a property.

Eight million women in the U.K. won the right to vote under the Representation of the People Act of 1918. But if women had been given full political equality with men, 21 million women would have been eligible to vote in the next parliamentary election.

There are many theories as to why the vote was given only to women over the age of thirty. Some historians believe the government still viewed younger women as too irresponsible to take voting seriously. Others believe that, because women outnumbered men and the government had no idea how women would vote, politicians were afraid of making women the voting majority in case it favored their opponents in the next general election.

Whatever the reason for not giving women full political equality with men in 1918, the British government had recognized it could no longer ignore the idea of women's suffrage.

In 1916, when her focus was on winning the war rather than winning the vote, Emmeline Pankhurst was asked about the suffragettes' campaign and replied, "We are like a dog that has buried a bone. They think we have forgotten all about it, but we've got the place marked."

The government feared that when eventually the war came to an end, the suffragettes would reignite their militant actions with an even greater ferocity than they had before.

The war had also highlighted the need to reform the voting qualifications for men. Thousands of men were away from home, fighting for long periods of time. This effectively disenfranchised them (meaning that they were disallowed from voting) because a man had to have lived at his registered address for the previous twelve months in order to qualify to vote.

And then there were the millions of working-class soldiers who had no right to vote in the first place because they did not own property. These two things would have resulted in many men fighting for a country in which they could not vote. Such clear injustice could not be allowed to continue.

"Votes for Heroes" became a popular campaign to change this situation, and to this some suffragists added "Votes for Heroines, Too!"

Many believed that giving British women the vote in 1918, albeit only to a select group, was the government's way of rewarding women for all their hard work and sacrifice during World War I.

Although the Representation of the People Act was a monumental victory for the suffragists and suffragettes, there wasn't much of a mood for celebration. The war was still raging and the casualties increasing.

War rumbled on for nine more months until it finally came to an end on November 11, 1918.

More than 800,000 British men were dead, and thousands of others were wounded.

It was in the aftermath of this horrific conflict that British women first went to the polling stations to vote in the general election on December 14, 1918.

It was a victory for the women who had been fighting for so long, but only a partial victory. Equal voting rights with men were still a long way off, and the campaign continued for another ten years.

1920: The Nineteenth Amendment

BY 1917, FIFTEEN STATES IN THE U.S. HAD GRANTED WOMEN THE RIGHT TO VOTE. MOST OF THESE WERE NEW STATES IN THE WEST WITH SMALL, MOSTLY MALE POPULATIONS, AND THEY HAD GRANTED WOMEN GREATER RIGHTS AS A WAY OF ENTICING THEM TO BECOME RESIDENTS.

But now the suffrage effort was stalled. The United States had entered World War I, and President Woodrow Wilson was distracted by the war effort from engaging with the suffrage question. Carrie Chapman Catt, then leading the National American Woman Suffrage Association (NAWSA), agreed to suspend her campaign to win the vote state-by-state and instead help with the war effort. Alice Paul and Lucy Burns, objecting to this decision and to Catt's strategy in general, led their recently formed National Woman's Party (NWP) in attention-getting protests, like picketing the White House, that were designed to force the president to consider a federal amendment to the Constitution that would make women's right to vote the law of the whole country.

When the picketers were arrested and jailed in miserable conditions, they, like their British counterparts, went on hunger strike. The forced feedings and threats of being locked in mental asylums—a long-favored societal strategy for getting rid of "difficult" women— won the sympathy of the public, as did the national organization's help with the war effort.

Congress and the president bowed to pressure at long last. In 1919, both houses of Congress voted for a Nineteenth Amendment to the Constitution, which said:

The right of citizens of the United States to vote shall not be denied or abridged by the United States or by any State on account of sex.

Congress shall have power to enforce this article by appropriate legislation.

But to become law, the amendment had to be ratified, or voted for, by the legislatures of three-fourths of the states. Now Catt's experience working state-by-state would come in handy again.

She was in Tennessee, deep in the reluctant South, lobbying its legislators when it became the crucial thirty-sixth state to vote for the amendment on August 20, 1920, by just 49 to 47. The amendment was ratified.

It is important to note that, although all women were granted the right to vote in 1920, many African American women were kept from doing so by taxes, literacy tests, and threats, all designed to keep them from having political influence. This was especially true in the South, where the legacy of slavery was a continued effort for control by white Southerners. It would take more than forty years for African American women to have a chance to fully exercise their legal rights, with the passage of the Voting Rights Act that struck down unfair local laws.

1928: Votes for All

WHEN THE QUALIFICATION OF WOMEN ACT BECAME LAW ON NOVEMBER 21, 1918, WOMEN IN THE U.K. COULD RUN FOR PARLIAMENT ON EQUAL TERMS WITH MEN AND BECOME MPS.

This meant that women could run for election at the age of twenty-one, but were still not permitted to vote until they were thirty! Despite this ridiculous contradiction, seventeen women ran for election in 1918. They included the great pioneers Christabel Pankhurst, Emmeline Pethick-Lawrence, and Charlotte Despard.

Only one woman was voted into Parliament that year. Constance Markievicz was elected to represent Dublin St. Patrick's, a constituency in Ireland, making her the first woman to win a seat in the House of Commons. At the time, Ireland was still ruled from Westminster, but because of the political struggle for Irish independence, Constance never actually came to London to take her seat in Parliament.

The following year, on December 23, 1919, the Sex Disqualification (Removal) Act became law. Professions and jobs that previously excluded women could no longer do so. This gave women access for the first time to careers as lawyers, accountants, magistrates, solicitors, or civil servants. By 1928, with women taking on increasingly important roles and even becoming MPs, the U.K. was more than ready for the long-overdue Equal Franchise Act.

Emmeline Pankhurst died on June 14, 1928. Just weeks later, the Equal Franchise Act was made law in the U.K., giving the vote to all women over the age of twenty-one.

Emmeline, after all her years of tirelessly campaigning to win votes for women, did not live to see this victory. But Millicent Fawcett, then eighty-one years old, was invited to Parliament to witness the new act pass into law. That evening, she wrote in her diary, "It is almost exactly sixty-one years ago since I heard John Stuart Mill introduce his (female) suffrage amendment to the Reform Bill on May 20th, 1867, so I have had extraordinary good luck in having seen the struggle from the beginning."

Five million more women became eligible to vote as a result of the Equal Franchise Act, which made women, at 52.7 percent, the voting majority over men.

There was not much opposition to the new law. Most people could see it was utter nonsense that women should be made to wait until they reached the age of thirty and meet the appropriate property qualifications when all men could vote from the age of twenty-one, or nineteen for men serving in the military. (The voting age was reduced to eighteen for both men and women in 1969.)

The general election of 1929 was the first in which women aged twenty-one to twenty-nine could vote. The number of female MPs rose to fourteen, and the Labor politician Margaret Bondfield became the first female Cabinet Minister.

Although women's place in society had taken a gigantic leap forward since the first Great Reform Act of 1832, the Equal Franchise Act of 1928 was only one step toward balancing the many inequalities that still existed between women and men.

The fight for women's suffrage was a fight to win the parliamentary vote, but it was also about changing the view of women in society: not just how society viewed women, but how women viewed themselves.

The suffragists and suffragettes in the United Kingdom and the United States knew that by putting women at the very heart of politics and giving them a political voice, they could change the old repressive, discriminatory perceptions of women and femininity and strive to achieve real gender equality.

The battle for full equality continues today, but through their tenacity and fearless determination, the tireless campaigners for women's suffrage had won a hugely important victory—for themselves and for the generations that followed.

A World of Suffrage

MERI TE TAI MANGAKĀHIA (1868–1920)
A campaigner for women's suffrage in New Zealand, she was the first woman to address the Maori political assembly, asking that women be allowed to vote for, and run as, members of the Maori parliament.

BRÍET BJARNHÉÐINSDÓTTIR (1856–1940)
An early supporter of women's liberation, she was the first Icelandic woman to write a newspaper article (on women's rights). She founded Iceland's first women's magazine and the first women's suffrage society.

FUSAE ICHIKAWA (1893–1981)
A teacher and journalist who later became a politician, she was an avid women's suffrage supporter. In 1918 she organized the New Woman's Association and in 1924 founded the Women's Suffrage League of Japan.

SAROJINI NAIDU (1879–1949)
The first Indian woman to be president of the Indian National Congress, she was called the Nightingale of India for the beautiful poetry she wrote. She helped found the Women's India Association in 1917.

LIN ZONGSU (1878–1944)
She formed the Women's Suffrage Comrades Alliance in 1911, the first organization of its kind in China, and established a journal, *Women's Time,* to publish information about suffrage.

DORIA SHAFIK (1908–1975)
A principal leader of the Egyptian women's liberation movement, she published a magazine focusing on women's issues in order to encourage Egyptian women to have an effective role within society.

MEENA KESHWAR KAMAL (1956–1987)
While still a student, she established the Revolutionary Association of the Women of Afghanistan to help promote equality for women, and she later founded the bilingual magazine *Women's Message.*

MELITTA MARXER (1923–2015)
In 1968 she formed the Committee for Women's Suffrage in Liechtenstein. In 1983, she and others spoke in front of the Council of Europe, bringing the international spotlight to their fight.

Bibliography

BOOKS

Atkinson, Diane. *The Suffragettes in Pictures*. Stroud, U.K.: History Press, 2010.

Bartley, Paula. *Access to History: Votes for Women*. London: Hodder, 2007.

Conkling, Winifred. *Votes for Women! American Suffragists and the Battle for the Ballot*. Chapel Hill, NC: Algonquin Young Readers, 2018.

Dooley, Chris. *Redmond: A Life Undone*. Dublin: Gill & Macmillan, 2015.

Flexner, Eleanor, and Ellen Fitzpatrick. *Century of Struggle: The Woman's Rights Movement in the United States*. Cambridge, MA: Belknap Press of Harvard University Press, 1996.

Owens, Rosemary Cullen. *A Social History of Women in Ireland, 1870–1970*. Dublin: Gill & Macmillan, 2005.

Phillips, Melanie. *The Ascent of Woman: A History of the Suffragette Movement and the Ideas Behind It*. London: Abacus Publishing, an imprint of Little, Brown, 2003.

Tickner, Lisa. *The Spectacle of Women: Imagery of the Suffrage Campaign, 1907–14*. Chicago: University of Chicago Press, 1988.

Traister, Rebecca. *Good and Mad: The Revolutionary Power of Women's Anger*. New York: Simon & Schuster, 2018.

Zimet, Susan, and Todd Hasak-Lowy. *Roses and Radicals: The Epic Story of How American Women Won the Right to Vote*. New York: Viking Books for Young Readers, 2018.

ARTICLES

Baker, Lee D. "Ida B. Wells-Barnett and Her Passion for Justice." Duke University website. April 1996. http://people.duke.edu/~ldbaker/classes/aaih/caaih/ibwells/ibwbkgrd.html.

Cohen, Danielle. "This Day in History: The 1913 Women's Suffrage Parade." *The White House: President Barack Obama* (blog). The White House archives, March 3, 2016. https://obamawhitehouse.archives.gov/blog/2016/03/03/this-day-history-1913-womens-suffrage-parade.

"Her Life." The National Susan B. Anthony Museum and House website. http://susanbanthonyhouse.org/her-life/#suff.

Holler, Deborah R. "The Remarkable Caroline G. Parker Mountpleasant, Seneca Wolf Clan," *Western New York Heritage*, Spring 2011.

"Japanese Actress Is Here to Study the Feminist Movement." *Star Tribune*, May 26, 1918. Reprinted at Newspapers.com. https://www.newspapers.com/clip/10051072/komaku_kimura_1918/.

Lewis, Jone Johnson. "International Woman Suffrage Timeline: Winning the Vote for Women Around the World." ThoughtCo. Last modified January 4, 2018. https://www.thoughtco.com/international-woman-suffrage-timeline-3530479.

Michals, Debra (ed.). "Sojourner Truth." National Women's History Museum website. Last modified 2015. https://www.womenshistory.org/education-resources/biographies/sojourner-truth.

"National Association of Colored Women." National Women's History Museum website. Last modified November 3, 2015. http://www.crusadeforthevote.org/nacw.

Parker, Lonnae O'Neal. "100 Years After Suffrage March, Activists Walk in Tradition of Inez Milholland." *Washington Post*. February 27, 2013. https://www.washingtonpost.com/entertainment/museums/100-years-after-suffrage-march-activists-walk-in-tradition-of-inez-milholland/2013/02/27/532872c0-7f7a-11e2-b99e-6baf4ebe42df_story.html?utm_term=.2e9eebdc6520.

"Sarojini Naidu." Cultural India. Last modified December 30, 2016. https://www.culturalindia.net/leaders/sarojini-naidu.html.

"Sojourner Truth: A Life of Legacy and Faith." Sojourner Truth Institute of Battle Creek website. Last modified 2018. https://sojournertruth.org/sojourner-truth.

"The Trailblazers." *The Black Suffragist* film website. Last modified March 30, 2016. http://www.blacksuffragette.com/.

"The Women Suffrage Timeline" Women Suffrage and Beyond. Last modified February 18, 2012. http://womensuffrage.org/?page_id=69.

Wagner, Sally Roesch. "The Untold Iroquois Influence on Early Radical Feminists: An intrepid historian tracks down the source of their revolutionary vision." *On the Issues Magazine*, Winter 1996. https://www.ontheissuesmagazine.com/1996winter/winter1996_WAGNER.php.